MY LIFE:

FACT IS
STRANGER
THAN FICTION

MY LIFE:

FACT IS
STRANGER
THAN FICTION

NORMAN RUBIN

Library of Congress Control Number:		2023919513
ISBN:	Hardcover	979-8-3694-0967-1
	Softcover	979-8-3694-0966-4
	eBook	979-8-3694-0965-7

Print information available on the last page.

Rev. date: 11/07/2023

To order additional copies of this book, contact:
Xlibris
844-714-8691
www.Xlibris.com
Orders@Xlibris.com
855838

Contents

A Ghost Story

A short true story about a real life experience.
Written Jan 26th, 2015

Both my wife and I are pragmatic realists, and have always been. During our lifetime we have heard many stories from friends, or have seen programs on television, that relate to stories of the supernatural. As a youngster, I recall watching two fascinating TV series entitled "Tales of Tomorrow" and "Twilight Zone", the latter program being hosted by Rod Serling who both introduced the half hour program, and provided a short comment on that night's tale after its conclusion. The stories we heard and the TV programs we watched were both interesting and entertaining. We took the TV programs as being purely fiction, and questioned the validity of stories that we heard told to us by people we knew. We never took any of them seriously until something happened to us one night a few years ago that made us re-think our position on the supernatural.

My wife and I owned a small vacation home in the Pocono Mountains of Pennsylvania in a small town known as Pocono Pines. Our tiny cabin is located in a community of homes known as Lake Naomi, just off state route 940, just a few miles from Mount Pocono. Since our cabin is in a heavily wooded area filled with deer, rabbits, wild turkeys, and birds, it is a very quiet and restful place to escape to since it lets us drop out of the world and just "unwind" for a little while. It was on warm a weekend in June, while we were at our little cabin, that something extraordinary happened.

On Saturday night of this particular weekend, my wife and I decided to turn in early and were in bed by about 11PM. We usually stayed up to catch the local news on TV and get the weather report for the next few days, but on this particular night we were quite tired so we skipped the news and got into bed just before 11PM. We were a bit uneasy during this particular weekend because about a month earlier, Judy's father Sol, had entered a hospice facility in Florida, and was clearly not in the best of health. Earlier that week, we received word from my wife's sister Beth, who also lived in Florida, not far where her dad was, that Sol was not doing very well and that his days on this planet were numbered. Our cabin is on an unlighted street and unless the moon is full, it is usually pitch dark in our cabin when our lights are out. On this particular evening, there was no moon, so it was so dark in our bedroom that we couldn't even see our own hands in front of our faces.

I recall having fallen asleep rather quickly, when I awoke to hear voices that seemed to be coming from the next room. I reached over to nudge Judy only to find that she was not there. I got out of bed, reached for a bathrobe, and opened the bedroom door that led to our all purpose room. The light was on and Judy was on the phone speaking to her sister Beth. Her sister had called to inform Judy that she had just received a call from Sol's hospice to inform her that their dad had just passed away. When Judy got off the phone she told me that the hospice had told Beth that Sol had died at 11:45 PM, about ¾ of an hour after we had gone to bed. After getting back into bed, Judy told me that something had happened just after we had gone to bed that initially I passed off as just a coincidence

Judy said that shortly after we had gone to bed, she was awakened by a cold breeze in our dark bedroom. Although we sleep with our windows open at night during the warm summers, on that particular night there was no wind and it was extremely quiet. After being awakened by the unusual cool breeze and opening her eyes, she said that she saw a faint white shadow of her father at the foot of our bed. The shadow appeared on the right, near the bedroom door, and slowly seemed to drift from right to left toward the single window that is to the left of our bed. When the white shadow reached the window, it just seemed to fade out. At that moment, Judy said she had the strange feeling that her dad had died. She glanced over at the illuminated clock on the small table next to our bed and noticed that it read 11:15PM. After telling me about her "vision" we both closed our eyes and drifted off to sleep since there was nothing much we could do until we heard further from Judy's sister regarding arrangements for their dad. We were just drifting off into "la-la land" when, at about midnight, the phone rang again, and Judy got up to take the call. It was Beth calling again with some more news regarding the passing of their dad.

She had called because she had been in contact with the hospice regarding making decisions on what to do next. The doctor that had examined Sol shortly after his passing, had filled out the certificate of death and the hospice wanted Beth to know some of the particulars on the certificate. Judy almost dropped the phone when Beth told her that the time of death listed on the certificate was exactly 11:15PM! This coincided exactly with the time that Judy had seen the faint white shadow move across our bedroom.

Needless to say, we did not sleep much that night. Of greater significance is that from that point on, so called "fantastic" stories dealing with the supernatural, took on a whole new meaning for us.

A Lifetime of Picking Wild Blueberries

1/22/12 (rev 100523)

It all started in the late 1940's shortly after my grandparents sold their small hotel that was located about 5 miles from the small town of Liberty NY, and retired to a small home about 3/4 mile from center of Liberty. Each summer, starting in 1947, I had the opportunity to get away from the August heat of the Bronx, where I lived with my parents and younger brother in a small two room apartment near the Bronx Zoo, and spend two wonderful weeks around the time of my birthday in August, in the cooler, fresh country air, visiting with my grandparents.

A tradition each summer, during my two week visit, was for my grandparents to take me, a cousin and sometimes an aunt and uncle, up to a place called the Cooley Mountain area just outside of Parksville, where wild blueberries grew and were there for the picking. My grandmother would usually pack a small lunch for us and we would head for the wild blueberry fields with straw baskets in hand to search for bushes laden with ripe fresh blueberries and fill the baskets with blueberries. My grandfather, who usually wore a straw hat to protect his bald head from the sun, would usually wander off on his own for hours and come back late in the day with the most (and biggest) blueberries.

The next day, I would help my grandmother, who was a great cook, bake blueberry pies and "putting up" blueberry preserves that she would use throughout the winter and spring. I can still smell the berries simmering in large pots on her stove, and taste the freshly made blueberry pie that I would love to have with cold milk.

My last visit to my grandparents in Liberty was in 1956. The following winter they decided to sell their home in Liberty and move back to Brooklyn to live with my aunt and uncle. Interestingly, they had started their lives in the USA exactly 50 years earlier after immigrating from the Ukraine in Russia to start a new life in Brooklyn before leaving the city to live on a farm they bought in Liberty. My blueberry picking summers with my grandparents ended when they moved back to Brooklyn since wild blueberries don't grow in Brooklyn.

My next encounter with wild blueberries was in the summer of 1963 when my wife and I decided to venture north to New England and spend a few days vacationing in Bar Harbor, Maine. The day before we arrived at our cabin just outside of Bar Harbor, a heavy fog moved in just as we crossed the bridge in our 1956 chevy from the mainland to Mount Dessert Island on our way to Bar Harbor. The fog was so thick that I could hardly see the line in the center of the highway. We managed to find our cabin, unpacked and went to bed. We awoke the next morning to a crystal clear day and, as I peered out of the rear window of our small cabin, I could see Cadillac Mountain about five miles away. Shortly after breakfast, I went out for a short walk and, much to my surprise, I found wild "low bush" blueberries growing on the grounds surrounding our cabin. Excitedly, I ran back into the cabin, got a small metal pot from the kitchen and, within a half hour or so, filled it with fresh blueberries. We stopped at a small market in Bar Harbor later in the day, picked up some sour cream, and had freshly picked blueberries and cream for dessert. I later found out that blueberries grow wild all over northern New England, especially in Maine.

Two years later, in the summer of 1965, my wild blueberry picking adventures began again while I was vacationing in Maine with my family. We were staying on Rangely Lake in a small rented cabin when we discovered, much to our surprise, that blueberries grew wild in the fields that surround the lake, particularly along the road that leads to Saddleback Mountain. Each summer, while vacationing in Rangely, we would always set aside a day or two to visit the fields where the wild blueberry bushes grew and pick blueberries with our kids. Our dog Winky always came with us and loved frolicking in the fields and eating the berries right off the lower growing (young) blueberry bushes. We would stop in the town of Rangely on the way back to our cabin, and pick up sugar so that we could prepare jars of blueberry preserves, just like my grandmother used to do. It was a family affair that everyone loved. Judy, my wife would also set aside several cups of berries and would prepare a blueberry pie, also so like my grandmother did.

We picked blueberries with our family in Rangely for almost 25 years, but stopped going to Rangeley after 1989 when we bought a small cabin in the Pocono Mountains. Our cabin in the Poconos became our new vacation "getaway" place. In the summer of 1990, while I was riding my bicycle in our Pocono community, I passed a small bog about a half mile from our cabin. Out of curiosity, I got off my bike and wandered into the bog, just to explore. After hiking a short distance from the road, I noticed a familiar looking bush that was loaded with small bright bluish looking berries. It was a wild blueberry bush growing right there in the bog. I walked I bit further into the bog and discovered that there were blueberry bushes growing all over the place, many loaded with ripe blueberries. I picked a few berries and discovered that they were extremely sweet. I ran back to my bike and pedaled as fast as I could back to our cabin to share my discovery with my wife Judy. We grabbed some pots and returned to the bog to pick several quarts of berries that we took back to our cabin and proceeded to follow our past tradition and process the fresh berries into blueberry preserves and pies.

This tradition has continued up to the present. We still have our little cabin in the Poconos where, each summer, from mid-July into August, I wander into the bog and pick the ripe wild blueberries that Judy and I cook on our stove in the cabin and make preserves and pies. We also freeze some berries for use in pancakes and muffins.

Each summer, when I go into the bog to pick berries near our cabin, I always recall the times I spent with my grandparents each summer at their small home outside of Liberty and the fun we had picking wild blueberries, making preserves and eating the fresh blueberry pie my grandmother had made. That was over 60 years ago, but it seems like just yesterday.

Introduction: A Lifetime Of Experiences And Memories

———————————— ❧ ————————————

9/07/23

About ten years ago, after contemplating my age and the fact that most of my life is history, I decided to start writing a series of articles entitled "My Life: Fact Is Stranger Than Fiction". This was prompted not only by my age, but the fact that I have had, as many people have, a very interesting life. Starting as a youth and continuing as a married man with my wife Judy with whom I have shared over 68 years, I have had many interesting experiences and have accomplished a great deal, both in my private life and as a professional electrical engineer. I have been to many interesting places, met interesting and sometimes important people, and have seen some incredibly beautiful sights, like the Grand Canyon, the Canadian Rockies, and the glacial fiords of the Alaskan coast.

During breakfast this morning at our little "get away" cabin in the Pocono Mountains of Pennsylvania, my wife and I were reflecting over our lives, the many people we have met and the places we have been to. Even though we have been here (on this planet) for only about 83 years, it was enlightening (to say the least), to reflect on these experiences, and the number of people we have known, the relationships we have or had, and the places we were fortunate to have visited.

Each of us travels a unique path in this thing we call life. By writing these true stories about my real life experiences it is prompting me to bring up memories of things that I have not thought about in many years and to correlated things that I never thought went together. Writing these articles is also helping me to expand my writing skills, and quite frankly, I am having a ball doing it.

An additional plus to this activity is that someday, my children will inherit this computer and my memory sticks and perhaps will open these files and read some or all of these true stories about my life. Many of the things I am writing about took place before our kids were born, and they will be new to them. Some of the things I am documenting, they experienced while they lived and traveled with us, but may not have been aware of my personal reaction to these experiences simply because we each see things differently. Other experiences covered in these short true stories occurred after they left our nest to attend school or started raising their own families (all three of our kids are married and each have two kids of their own).

An additional plus is that after sharing some of the stories I have written with others, they often say: "What are you going to do with these wonderful stories? Are you thinking about publishing them?" So many folks have expressed an interest in reading the collection of memoirs that I am writing, that I have decided to publish a book with a collection of some of these stories, so what you are holding is it.

Because of the fun I am having documenting my life's stories, and what a rewarding project it is turning out to be, I would like to encourage anyone reading this to consider sitting down at a computer or taking out a pen and notepad and starting to write about their own lives. It is my belief, and hope, that you will experience what I am experiencing while engaging in this activity of creative writing and perhaps have as much fun as I am.

A Wonderful Life

101320

I was born in the Bronx on August 14,1940 in Prospect Hospital. Ahead of me was a life waiting to be filled with adventures that at present seem incredible.

I got off to a fast start, and was walking and talking by the age of 1. I suspect I inherited the genes of the Rubin family since my grandparents, who had immigrated to the USA from the Ukraine in 1906, were highly creative and intelligent. This was also true of my aunts and uncles on the Rubin side of the family. My grandparents fled Russia because of the pogroms that were prevalent at that time. I often say in jest that they fled from a little town called Anitefka (the ficticous small town in the play "Fiddler On the Roof").

I was and still am very curious and my mother said that the first word I uttered was "why". When I was four years old, my dad bought me a metal wind up train set. When he came home from work the day after giving me this wonderful gift, he got very upset when he found that I had taken it apart. When he asked me why I ruined the train set, I told him I wanted to see if there were people in the train cars. Of course we were both upset because there were no people inside.

I started school at P.S. 6 in the Bronx, about a block and a half from where I was living, and by the time I made it to the first grade, I had a title- "The Holy Terror Of P.S. 6." I was not physical, but had the bad habit of disrupting the class I was in. When I tell people who know me about this, they say that I was bored with what was going on in school, hence, I found ways to make my life interesting, by fooling around. Of course, my teachers were not very fond of me since it was a real challenge for them.

At around this time I started developing an interest in magnetism and light. There was a store on Tremont Avenue, a few blocks from where I lived, that sold things like magnets and prisms, so I saved a few cents from my allowance and bought these things to play with. When I was eight, my dad bought me a Lionel train set. This sparked my interest in model railroading. This interest continued into my adult years during which I also started collecting and running HO trains, that were much smaller than the O gauge Lionel trains. If you check the Olinville Junior High School year book, you will see the words: "train crazy" next to my name.

I attended Evander Childs High School, also in the Bronx, and became highly interested in math and physics. When I graduated, in the spring of 1958, I received an award for achievement in physics.

At the age of eleven, I became interested in the growing field of electronics, and I started building kits sold by Allied Radio and HeathKit. These included audio amplifiers and radio transmitters. I recall designing and building an electric eye that could activate a small relay when a beam of light was interrupted.

There used to be an electronics store called Lafayette Radio located on Fordham Road, across the street from Fordham University. I used to go there and buy parts to "mess around with" at home. The men there used to chat with the kids and adults that came there to by parts and answer questions about all sorts of things in electronics and radio.

The fall of 1955 marked a turning point in my life since it was at Evander that I met a young girl who was only 14. Her name was Judy Herman. Little did I know back then that we were to become husband and wife and spend the rest of our lives together. We started "going together" in November, and except for a small interlude in the summer of 1956, continued as boy and girlfriend till our wedding in June of 1962.

In the fall of 1958 I started my college education at CCNY and Judy started on her BA in Math at Hunter College in the Bronx. Four years later she graduated and landed a job at my old JHS, Olinville, and I continued for another 6 months at CCNY and graduated in January of 1963 with a degree in Electrical Engineering.

My first job was working for a small company in Westbury long Island called Digital Electronics. Over the next 43 years I worked for eleven companies and applied my skills as an electronics engineer in many different areas including Radar, Sonar, Bio-medical engineering, data encryption, electrostatics, and the special needs field.

In 1966, 2 1/3 years after our first daughter Joy was born, we decided to leave New York and start a new life in Bucks County Pennsylvania. I also changed my specialty from Sonar work to the bio-medical field and worked for a year for a small department of Norden called Telemedics. Unfortunately, the company decided to move the bio-medical engineering dept. to Connecticut and I ended up working in the Sonar field again.

In 1968 I started working for a small company in Cheltenham called General Atronics, and was there for 10 years. I did some very challenging work including leading the team that designed the voice communication for the NASA Space Shuttle. I also was the team leader that pioneered the technology that is now in everything from cell phones to your TV set and virtually anything that uses electronics. I left this company in 1978 and joined a medium sized company called AEL, in Lansdale, PA. While there I did some very interesting work including designing some very special circuits that helped Boeing develop the 757 and 767 aircraft.

During my summer vacations, we discovered New England and traveled to New Hampshire and then to Rangeley Maine. We fell in love with Rangeley, and vacationed there almost every summer until 1987, staying in housekeeping cottages for two weeks, usually in mid-summer.

We continued to take vacations in the summer, and traveled all over the country with our family that had grown to five, since we had two more daughters. Our kids were all born between 1964 and 1969 and even to this day, have fond memories of our family trips and vacations, particularly, our vacations in Rangeley, Maine.

In 1989, we decided to purchase a small cabin in the Poconos, and this became our retreat. It was only 2 hours from our home in Churchville, PA, and was winterized, so that we were able to use it year round. I set up a computer in one corner of our all purpose room and was able to type over ninety memoirs like this one. I also did my landscape painting there as well as the preparation of many of my power point presentations. I have a series of sixteen presentations that I give at places like the public libraries throughout Bucks and Montgomery Counties, and senior centers in Philadelphia, Bucks County, Montgomery County, and the library in Pocono Pines.

As our kids got older, and started to live on their own, including getting married to three wonderful guys, Judy and I traveled as a couple to many interesting places that included Costa Rica, Mexico, Alaska, and most of our great national parks, including the Grand Canyon, Brice Canyon, Canyonlands, Yosemite, and of course, the Tetons and Yellowstone. We also discovered a great travel company called Viking, and did several river and ocean cruises in Europe with them. We also took three wonderful trips to Hawaii.

Because of my work as an engineer, I was able to travel all over the USA and into Canada primarily to provide instruction to facilities that had purchased new equipment that I had designed. I usually tried to plan a trip so that I had a weekend over which I could visit places of interest in the area that I was visiting. I spent a great deal of time on the west coast and traveled to Washington, Oregon, San Francisco, Los Angeles and San Diego. My work also took me to Texas, Omaha, Florida, New York State, Pennsylvania, Georgia, and the Carolina's.

My last position was working for a non-profit company known then as The Woods School, that provided care and housing for people of all ages with mental and physical challenges. I was hired to start a new department called The Squire Assistive Technology Center that enabled me to use my extensive experience as an engineer to help many people with special needs. This was the best job I ever had since I was helping people live better lives using my skills as an electrical engineer. I retired from this position in 2006 but continued to provide services for seven special needs private clients off campus. I am still engaged in this work as a private consultant and provide services via my consulting company called Noran Technical Consultants. I can never thank CCNY enough for the education I received for free, and was able to change the world by making things better for us all.

In 2019, my wife and I decided that our home in Churchville had too many challenges (stair cases), so se decided to move to an over 65 retirement community called Pennswood Village. It was only about fifteen minutes from our home in Churchville, so it enabled us to stay close to our family and friends. We spend most of our time in our wonderful apartment in PWV but still travel to the Poconos to spend time at our cabin.

In summary, we have had a very long and wonderful life. Although we face more and more physical challenges as we approach the twilight of our lives, Judy and I, who have shared 67 years together, look forward to being able to still travel, visit with family and friends, and continue to enjoy life.

All The Things I Grew

100523

When I was twelve years old, my parents moved from a tiny apartment in the central Bronx, a few blocks from the world famous Bronx Zoo, to the northeast Bronx known as the Edenwald Section, and my life changed.

They bought a small semi-attached (two side by side living units) that had two bedrooms, a single bathroom, a living room, kitchen and dining room, and a garage and basement. Most importantly, it had a small back yard with a small area of earth. We moved into this home in mid-winter of 1952, but when the spring came, I decided to buy some seeds and grow some flowers and vegetables. My dad also planted a maple tree toward the rear of our property that gave us some shade. If I recall, I grew some zinnia, marigold, ageratum, and tomatoes, peppers, cabbage and lettuce. It was the second time I had the opportunity to garden. My first time was when I was in grade school at P.S. 6 and we had a small garden known as a Victory Garden.

After I got married in1962, my wife Judy and I moved into a nice apartment just off Gun Hill Road, about a mile from our high school, Evander Childs, where we first met.

We lived in this apartment for four years, but then moved to lower Bucks County where we lived in a very nice garden apartment in Trevose. We lived on the ground floor and had a tiny patio that gave us the opportunity to grow some plants in small window boxes. A year later we moved into our semi-custom house in Churchville, not foo far from Trevose. This home was on a builders half acre (twenty thousand square feet). The home occupied about 1000 square feet, leaving about nineteen thousand for lawn, flower beds, and a vegetable garden.

Over the next few years, I bought many trees and planted them all around our house. On the east and west borders, I planted pine trees, and then planted both fruit and shade trees on various spots around the house. I had three apple trees, three cherry trees, two peach tree, an apricot tree, two pear trees, and ten blueberry bushes. Unfortunately, I quickly learned that there were many insects, birds and diseases that loved these fruit trees and bushes and over the next ten years or so, I lost most of them. Some survived, but lived out their lives and eventually died of old age. The trees that survived included a maple tree, oak tree, a decorative cherry tree, the blueberry bushes, and many azalea bushes. We loved our fruit trees and harvested the fruit to eat raw, or make pies and preserves. Our cherry tree, a Montmorency, was a sour cherry, that made great pies, and preserves. It survived for about thirty years but eventually died of old age.

Unfortunately, we learned that the birds also loved many of the fruits that our trees and bushes produced, particularly the cherries and blueberries. We were forced to try many different things to keep the birds away, but they are pretty smart, so the things we tried seldom were effective. As a result, we found that were faced with an ongoing battle with mother nature if we wanted to harvest the fruits of our labor. The bottom line was that we finally gave up and let the fruit trees and bushes either die of old age or damage caused by insects or disease. The blueberry bushes survived until we finally sold our home after living in it for 52 years.

On a more positive note, I did have a vegetable garden for about 30 years until my neighbors maple tree grew to about 50 feet tall and shaded my 1000 sq. ft. vegetable garden. The shade was so dense that virtually nothing would grow there except ground ivy that I planted there just as a ground cover.

I did continue to grow many flowering plants that included bulbs like tulips and daffodils, as well as dahlias that grow from tubers. Each spring I would order these, many of which were shipped from Holland. I also ordered seeds from both Parks and Burpee that enabled me to grow flowering plants like zinnia, marigold, ageratum, coxcomb, Chinese forget-me-nots, and foxglove. We had many years of wonderful experiences with these colorful plants that enabled us to make cut flower arrangements for use in our house.

In 2019 we moved into an apartment in an over 65 community and hence, my gardening efforts would have to be significantly cut back. Fortunately, this community did have a vary large garden area in an open field that gave me the opportunity to continue gardening. Over the summer of 2020, I grew both flowers and vegetables on a single 25' X 25' garden plot. I grew zinnia, marigold, dusty miller, ageratum, and dahlias. I also grew corn, peppers, and tomatoes. Our tomato crop consisted of about 16 plants that I purchased from a farm store near where we used to live in Churchville. We harvested about

250 delicious tomatoes over the summer and into the fall. We ate them at lunch and dinner in salads, and also cooked them for storage in sterilized jars so that they could be enjoyed in dishes like macaroni and cheese, Spanish omlets, as well as other dishes.

In summary, I have been gardening for 71 of my 83 years, and hope to continue gardening in our community garden for as long as I can. It has enabled us to enjoy both the beauty of the trees and flowers that I grew, and the excellent taste of home grown fruits and vegetables. I never used chemical sprays, so that as well as tasting well, what we ate was also healthy. Our three children reaped the benefits of what I grew and also enjoyed many years of excellent meals that we prepared from what we grew. A side benefit of my planting efforts was to turn a builders bare half acre into something that provided vegetables, beautiful trees some of which bore fruit, and flowers. In short, my efforts helped make our planet a bit greener.

A Strange Thing Happened
At Watkins Glen

11/10/22

My wife Judy and I were married in June of 1962 and decided to honeymoon in Watkins Glen. It is a beautiful succession of cascading waterfalls located about 150 miles west of New York City. We parked the car and proceeded to walk along the stone path that leads upward through the glen. Being an amateur photographer, I stopped frequently to take pictures using my 35 mm slide camera. It was a cool misty day, and it had rained the night before, and while there, we met no others in the glen. After passing the last waterfall, we followed the stream that feeds the glen, crossing several small bridges that straddle the stream. We then crossed the last bridge and followed the stone walkway that leads to a stone staircase that leads to the ridge of the glen. As we reached the staircase we stopped and stared in amazement at a large fresh chalk heart that was drawn on the stone wall. There was arrow across the heart but written within the heart were two names. The two names were "Norm & Judy". To this day, Judy and I are still wondering who drew the heart and put our names in it. Remember the title of this collection of memoirs; "My Life: Fact Is Stranger Than Fiction".

"A Visitor From Another World"

4/12/2010

In the summer of 1980, my wife, three children and I decided to spend our two week summer vacation in Parry Sound, Canada, at a small fishing camp on Georgian Bay, about 80 miles north of Toronto. The bay is noted for having crystal clear water, thousands of small islands, and great fishing. It is particularly noted for its muskellunge, a very large aggressive fighting fish with very sharp teeth. My wife's sister and husband Gary, with their 18 month old son joined us on this vacation and met us at "Camp Wawanaisa", the cabin colony we stayed at.

While vacationing at Camp Wawanaisa, we met several other families who chose this particular vacation camp for their summer get-away. One of the folks we met was Jim, a postal worker from Toronto, who came to Georgian Bay to relax and try his hand at fishing for muskellunge. As the first week progressed and we got to know Jim better, we learned that he was interested in renting a small powered boat and spending an entire day on the water. Since Gary and I had similar plans, the three of us decided to get away together for a day exploring the islands in the bay, and trying our luck at fishing for muskellunge.

We picked a beautiful clear sunny day with temperatures in the mid-70's for our day on the water. We explored several of the islands that were within 10 miles or so of our camp, ate our packed lunch on one of the islands, and then swam in the crystal clear (but very cold) water surrounding that island. We fished on and off throughout the day, but none of us were lucky enough to even get a nibble.

As nightfall approached and the sun dipped below the horizon, we packed our gear and started heading back to camp. The wind, that was barely noticeable during the day, had stopped completely, the sky was a beautiful deep azure color, and the water was as smooth as glass. As our open boat headed slowly southeast for our return to Wawanaisa, the blue of the sky continued to darken, and the stars slowly began to appear in the cloudless Canadian sky.

It was now about 9PM and, as we headed back to the dock, Gary, my brother-in-law, was handling the motor at the stern, Jim was in the center on one of the seats, and I was at the bow, lying on some floatation cushions gazing up at the stars, the discussion shifted to how small our planet is, and how highly likely it is that there are other intelligent life forms on other planets somewhere up there in the sky.

As we were nearing the end of this discussion which lasted for several minutes and focused on the possibility of non-earthlings occupying our vast universe, suddenly, and without warning, the star studded sky, that was quite dark by now, was brightened by a white glowing object due east of us and very close to the horizon. We all saw it and watched it in silence as the object, which clearly was not an airplane or helicopter, and was clearly larger and brighter than any star, traveled from east to west across the clear, cloudless sky. At its peak, when it was due north of us, the object was about 30 degrees above the horizon and appeared to be moving at a constant speed and in a straight line. Its tail was also clearly visible and extended to the east in a smooth continuous arc of about 25 degrees or about 1/6th of the sky. The "head" of the bright white glowing object appeared to be burning, and pieces could be seen breaking off behind the head as the tail formed.

We were almost speechless at the sight of this object and that it (whatever it was) appeared during our discussion of the possibility of extraterrestrial life. When we got back to the dock we were all wondering if we had witnessed the approach and perhaps landing of a visitor from another world. Needless to say, we all had trouble sleeping that night pondering what we had all seen and what it might have been.

The following morning, Jim, our fishing companion, and witness to our suspected ET sighting, called Toronto only to discover to our joint disappointment, that what we had seen in the night sky the evening before, was also seen by millions of people in North America and Canada and was not a visitor from another planet. What we had all seen was only an old Russian satellite that had fallen back to earth and disintegrated as it entered earths atmosphere. Even though we had not witnessed a visitor from outer space, our observance was still an exciting and amazing coincidence.

"I'm Back To Where I Started Over 50 Years Ago"

April 13, 2016

In the early 1950's, the New York City school system introduced a new step in the progression from grade school to high school. It was called "Junior High School" and covered grades 7, 8 and 9, very similar to what is currently known as "Middle School" here in Pennsylvania. When this new system was introduced, I was living in the northeast Bronx near 233rd street and White Planes Road and was finishing the 6th grade at P.S. 87. In the fall of 1952, after completing the 6th grade, I entered Junior High School 113, also known as Olinville JHS, and had to take two different public buses to get to school.

Junior High School was a whole new world for me since, unlike public school up through grade 6, you stayed in one classroom and had one teacher for all subjects, we now "changed classes" as we moved from subject to subject as each school day progressed. As part

27

of the enriched education process inherent in the new JHS system, at least once each week, each student would report to the auditorium for a special class that usually entailed watching a film on some educational subject. These weekly film sessions usually lasted for the better part of an hour and were often followed by a short lecture given by a teacher on the subject matter of the film.

I quickly learned that the school had something known as an "audio/video squad" (simply known as the "A/V squad"), that consisted of a small select group of students, usually teenage boys like myself, that would be responsible for setting up and running the equipment that was used to show these weekly films. Since, as a teenager, I was highly interested in both sound recording and reproduction and movies, I volunteered to become a member of the A/V Squad and was responsible for showing these films to auditorium class sometimes as often as three times per week. My job was to pull down the huge screen on the auditorium stage, set up the two large loudspeakers, run up to the projection booth on the second floor, load the film onto the 16 millimeter sound projector, and adjust the projector so that the film and sound would be synchronized properly. On a visual cue from the teacher, I would hit the light switch to turn off the auditorium lights and start the projector. I was a member of the A/V Squad at Olinville for my full 3 years there until I graduated and went on to continue my education at Evander Childs High School.

We now jump forward about 55 years to the spring of 2010, and, as a result of a chance meeting with my friend to be, Max, I became a member of a very special group of mostly retired professionals known as REAP. The group relied on a laptop computer, a special computer projector and an audio system that utilized both wired and wireless microphones to enable its members to make presentations each week on a topic of their choosing. During my first meeting at REAP problems were encountered with the computer equipment and audio system that resulted in the presenter having to stop several times during the presentation so that the audio and visual systems could be adjusted to restore them to their proper working condition. Needless to say, neither the presenter nor the members were terribly happy with the unscheduled interruptions. From speaking with some of the REAP members, I quickly learned that these disruptions occurred on a fairly regular basis.

Since I had had some experience with computer based projection systems as well as audio amplifiers, speaker systems and public address systems, it occurred to me that I might be able to offer my services to the group to try to look into and possibly correct some of the problems that they were having that resulted in frequent disruptions of the presentations.

At the end of this first session that I had attended, I spoke to the president of REAP and offered to remove the intermittent wireless microphone system, take it home with me and look into why it was not functioning reliably. At home, I found that there were several internal problems with the system and proceeded to make the necessary adjustments and repairs. At the next REAP meeting, I set up the restored audio unit, and it performed flawlessly for the entire session.

Since I found REAP very enlightening and found its members quite interesting, I decided to join REAP the following fall. Because of my success in fixing the REAP presentation equipment and then setting it up and running it for the group, I was "elected" to become the A/V guy and proceeded to handle this job on a regular basis. In effect, I found that I had become the REAP "A/V Squad".

In reflecting over my life, it appears that things have gone full circle since I appear to be *back to where I started* earlier in my life when I volunteered to become a member of the Olinville JHS A/V squad way back in the 1950's when I still lived in the Bronx.

"Be Careful of What and Where you Draw"

— ❧ —

4/16/2010

In the mid-1950's, my uncle Joe got me summer job working for a commercial photo finishing company that was then known as Berkey Photo. Their processing plant and company headquarters were located in Manhattan on 13th street just west of 4th Avenue about one block from Union Square. At the time I worked for Berkey, they were the second largest photo finishing company in the the Unites States, with Kodak being number 1. I worked for Berkey Photo for four summers while I was in high school and college.

My first summer was spent in the black and white department sorting various sizes of photographic prints that had just come off a ferrotype drum that simultaneously dried the prints and applied the high gloss finish that was very popular at that time. This job was not very interesting or challenging, but it got me through the summer and helped me earn a few dollars to help get me through the winter.

The following summer, I worked in the color department getting rolls of transparency film, primarily ektachrome and anscochrome, ready to be developed. This too was not a terribly challenging job, but kept me busy through the summer and again helped me put a few dollars in the bank. When I started working in the factory at Berkey, and discovered that more than half of my coworkers were Hispanic (mostly from Puerto Rico), I got very excited, because initially I felt that my summer job would give me a good opportunity to practice the Spanish I studied in both junior and high school. I quickly learned, much to my disappointment, that the language spoken by my Hispanic friends was not Castilian, as was taught in school. Further, they spoke much to fast for me to be able to follow, and the words they seemed to use most frequently, they don't teach in school!

During my third summer, purely by chance, someone in the office left on maternity leave creating a short time vacancy. As a result, I found my self moving up to ladder and no longer had to work in the factory, but was now surrounded by mostly young women who did the clerical and bookkeeping work for the company. The vacancy that I filled was a unique job that entailed sorting cash, checks and foreign currency (mostly Canadian bills and coins), preparing a total on an adding machine, and bundling it up for deposit in Berkey's bank account at a nearby bank. At the end of each day, usually in the late afternoon, it was also my responsibility to take the bundled deposits to the bank for processing by one of the tellers, and then returning to Berkey with the stamped deposit slips.

I generally arrived at the bank after it had closed to the general public and had to wait in the virtually empty bank for up to one hour while the teller verified that my deposits were correct. Since I enjoyed pencil sketching and had been drawing and painting with water color and colored pencils since I was a youngster, I would bring a pad and pencil with me to the bank and, instead of just sitting in the empty bank twiddling my thumbs, would generate pencil sketches of whatever came into my mind. The bank guard, who was always present while I was there, would generally wander over to see my sketches, and, on more than one occasion, would comment on how good they were.

On one occasion, in mid-july, after I had been going through this daily banking ritual for about three weeks, it occurred to me that it would be interesting to make a sketch of the bank as seen from where I was sitting. So, shortly after turning my deposits over to the teller, I picked up my pencil and started to sketch the interior of the bank.

As I was putting the finishing touches on my sketch and the teller was completing her accounting of my deposits, the bank guard drifted over to see what I was up to on that day. He took one look at the sketch, which I thought was quite good, and, instead of complimenting me, reached down, took my sketch of the bank, and abruptly, escorted me into the bank manager's office. It seems, after looking at my detailed sketch of the bank, neither the guard nor the bank president, seemed very impressed. For some reason that did not occur to me, they were rather annoyed with both me and my sketch. After consulting with the guard privately for a minute or so, the bank manager asked me why I was making a detailed drawing of the bank. After hearing my response, and apparently concluding that my intentions were very innocent, he returned the sketch to me and politely asked me not to make any more drawings of the bank.

When I got back to the office a few minutes later, the office manager escorted me to the corporate office area and I had the opportunity to meet the president of Berkey Photo, Ben Berkey himself. Apparently, while I was returning from the bank, the bank manager had been on the phone with Mr. Berkey discussing my talents as an artist. When I showed Mr. Berkey my sketch of the bank, for some reason, he did not seem too impressed either.

Well, for a short while, it looked like my summer job was going to end only a few short weeks after it started. Instead, after contemplating the situation for a short while, and talking to me briefly about my interests in drawing, and my age and background, in his infinite wisdom as president, he decided that no harm was done. He then kindly returned my sketch, and after instructing me to be more careful about what I sketched and where I sketched, let me return to the front office, where I finished the day, got on the subway, and returned home.

That evening when I discussed what had happened with my parents, they thought the whole incident was quite funny but agreed that when waiting in places like banks, it would be best not to make detailed sketches, particularly of the bank, but to just bring along a paperback novel and just sit there and read! So, for the remainder of the summer, while making my bank deposits for Berkey Photo, I left my sketching pad at the office and just read a good book or two, and left my sketching for other times and places.

Childhood Memories of Summer Nights in the Bronx

───────────────── ❧ ─────────────────

I have many fond memories of my childhood days in the Bronx, but most often, I recall the hot "dog days" of July and August, when twilight approached, and it was just simply to hot to stay indoors.

I was born in Prospect Hospital in the Bronx, in August of 1940, just as World War II was escalating and the war in the Pacific was yet to begin. By the mid-1940's both wars had ended, television was a just curiosity for most people, and people actually *listened to* boxing matches and baseball games on the radio.

At that time, I lived with my parents and younger brother, in a two room, ground floor apartment, of a five story walk-up (no elevator) building. Our tiny apartment was one of two buildings at 178th street and Vyse avenue, just a few blocks from the southern entrance to the Bronx Zoo. There were two sets of wide stairs in the front of the two buildings that led from the street to the courtyard that was on the upper level that led to the two entrances of our buildings. There was a small garden in the middle of the shared courtyard with a single, very large tree, most likely an oak or maple.

Since air conditioning was virtually unknown to those living in apartments, it was virtually impossible to remain indoors on these hot summer nights. After finishing dinner in the early evening before sunset, people of all ages would congregate in the front of our buildings and sit on the front steps or on folding chairs. There were the older folks either retired or close to it, mothers with infants in their baby carriages, and young or middle aged working men and women who had to get out of their apartments to get some relief from the heat. The adults would pass the time by reading books, newspapers or magazines, or playing games like cards, checkers or chess. It was fairly bright at night since the City of New York had the foresight to install a bright overhead street light right in front of our building. Although the adults had plenty of things to do to keep them busy, we kids had a problem: what to do the pass the time on these hot summer evenings?

To keep from getting into trouble, my friends and I engaged in variety of "makeshift" games that included sidewalk checkers, hide and seek, and a game called "Johnny-On-the-Pony". I learned in later life that this last game was known as "Buck-Buck" in Philadelphia. If it was still light enough, the boys would ride in the paved streets on steel wheeled roller skates that would attach to street shoes with metal clamps and a strap with a buckle. A special "skate key" would be used to tighten the metal clamps at the front of the skate. We would also play sidewalk ball with a "spaldine" (a pink rubber ball) or four corner ball in the street. Some of us had homemade "scooters" that were made from a vegetable shipping crate, a fence post board and a roller skate. We would keep busy with these various activities until late at night then, when it cooled down somewhat, go inside to go to bed and try to sleep.

By the late 1940's however, things began to change. I remember the Tolshinskys, on the third floor, being the first family in our building to get a television set. We would congregate in the evenings in their apartment, sit on their living room floor, and watch the small 12" black and white TV screen along with a dozen or so of our neighbors.

Tuesday nights were special since the *Lone Ranger* was on at 7:30, followed by Milton Berle and his *Texaco Star Theater*. Some of us even stayed after 9Pm to watch the *Molly Goldberg* show. Somehow, the heat of the summer did not deter us from staying indoors to watch TV in the evenings.

Within a few years, most of our neighbors bought their own TV sets, so gathering in the small living room of the Tolshinskys came to an end, since we could now stay in our own apartments and watch TV whenever we wanted. In those days, TV programming was not available 24/7 since most stations "signed off" at midnight and did not go back on the air till about 7AM. I can recall stations showing the American flag waving at midnight along with the star spangled banner, then the picture disappearing to be replaced my just noise. When the stations were ready to resume broadcasing in the morning, they would display a four armed "target" in black and white. When TV gradually replaced radio as we entered the fifties, the men no longer listened to boxing and baseball on the radio, but could actually watch boxing matches and baseball on the little TV screens. I remember those early days of TV, when watching the trotters at Yonkers Raceway and women competing in the "roller derby" were very popular. And how could I forget the wrestling matches with wrestlers' that had names like "Gorgeous George", "Man Mountain

Dean", and "Haystack Calhoun '. The gatherings outside of the building on hot summer nights slowly became a thing of the past. Little by little, the television set replaced the social gatherings in front of city buildings that were so common back then.

About fifteen years ago, we went back to visit our old neighborhood in the Bronx, but were shocked to discover that our building had been torn down along with neighboring buildings and were replace with a high-rise, low income housing project with 14 story buildings. The street we used to play in on those hot summer nights was gone. Tears came to my eyes when I realized that a memorable part of my childhood was gone forever. I guess the saying "you can never go back" is true. Those hot summer days in front of our building on 178th street live only in my memory now, and all too soon, it will be gone too.

Cortland Street & Union Square

11/1/15

On Sunday, October 25th 2015, REAP, the group I belonged to of Retired Executives and Professionals, took its fall one day bus trip to visit the World Trade Center Memorial Museum and in the afternoon, a visit to the newly opened Whitney museum. For me, this trip, although very enjoyable and educational, had a particular significance, since as a teenager and young adult, I actually made trips to Cortland Street, but also worked, for several summers while I was in high school and college, on or near Union Square, that is a short distance from both Canal and Cortland Streets.

I was born in the Bronx, and at about the age of 11 or so, developed an interest in electronics. Actually, I had interests in many things that included playing with light and sound, magnetism, astronomy and our solar system, photography, collecting vinyl records and listening to a wide range of types of music, the reproduction of sound (audio systems), gardening, and model railroading. In fact, this last interest, model railroading, resulted in my getting a Lionel train set, and building a significant train layout that occupied most of my time. If you check my Junior High School year book, next to my name, it actually says: "Train Crazy".

In the summer of 1956, my father, invested in a partnership with another individual whose focus was buying properties in Manhattan that served food and beverages to the public. One of their acquisitions was a small luncheonette known as the "Dineer" that was located on the corner of 15th street and 4th avenue, on the east side of Union Square. It just happened to be located across the street from the original S. Kleins discount department store, that was the forerunner of stores like K-mart and Wal-mart. I shopped at S. Kleins from 1956 until we left N.Y. and moved to Pennsylvania in 1966. Many of my LP records were purchased in their record department, and most of my clothes that I wore back then were purchased there.

Because of my working at the Dineer I began exploring the shopping areas not too far from Union Square. I soon discovered Canal and Cortland Streets where there were many stores that sold war surplus items of both an electrical and electronic nature, but also a wide range of mechanical stuff, also left over from the second world war. I helped out at the Dineer, and also delivered food orders for nickel and dime tips to the local office buildings mostly on and near Union Square. Most of these were on 4th avenue a short walk north of Union Square. We were busiest in the morning up to and including lunch time. By about 2PM things slowed down, and I often found myself with little to do. As a result, I would hop onto the subway at 14th street and take it for a few short stops south either to Canal or Cortland streets.

I would then wander from store to store, "checking out" the goodies that were on tables on the sidewalks in front of the stores and inside. I seldom came back "empty handed" and often got home with shopping bags full of electronic circuit boards, metal chassis, vacuum tubes, and other things to "play with". As a point of interest, Cortland Street was known as "Radio Row" back then because the stores sold electronic and radio equipment, vacuum tubes, and other items related to electronics and radio. A second interesting point is that the hi-fi field was basically "born" on Cortland Street. On one trip, about a year after meeting my girl friend and wife to be, Judy, I ran across a monaural hi-fi amplifier that I bought for about $15 around which I built a complete audio system with a VM (Voice of Music) automatic record player and an external speaker enclosure with a coaxial 8" speaker. I still have this system in the attic but am actually using the speaker that I have in our family room. Amazingly about 60 years after putting this system together, the speaker system still sounds like "brand new".

The following summer, 1957, by coincidence, my aunt Bea's new husband, Joe, happened to be manager at a commercial photofinishing company called Berkey Photo, that had its photofinishing plant on the ground floor and basement of an office building on 13th street, just off 4th avenue. Since I needed a job for the summer, and Joe was a manager at Berkey, he managed to get me a job working at Berkey in the black and white photo finishing department. My job for the entire summer was to process the black and white prints that were coming off two huge rotating "ferrotype" drums in large rolls about a foot in diameter, cut them into individual prints, inspect them for quality and proper exposure, emboss them, match up the finished sets of prints with the owners order bags, and place the finished orders in boxes to get them ready for delivery to both drug stores throughout the city as well as major department stores like Saks, Lord and Taylor, and S. Kleins. It was also my job to send orders back to the darkroom for reprinting of individual prints that I deemed to be not of sufficient quality to be sent to the customer.

Since Berkey Photo was located just one block off Union Square, I was able to continue visiting both Canal and Cortland streets after I finished work at the end of each day. I also recall making special trips on Saturdays, just to be able to shop at these great stores that provided me with "stuff" to keep me busy when not in school or engaged in other activities like flying kites, playing handball, flying a model airplane, or having fun with my Lionel Train set.

As things worked out, I actually worked for Berkey Photo for four summers, from 1957 to 1960 and continued my jaunts to Canal and Cortland Streets. My last summer spent working for Berkey was 1960, but by coincidence, in 1961, I ended up working for one of their competitors in the Bronx called Fotochrome. It was located on Washington Avenue, just off Tremont Avenue. I was there for two summers doing maintenance work on the machines that took the 35mm color slide film that had been processed and cut it into individual frames, placed them in cardboard slide mounts, and numbered and dated them. I was attending Engineering School at CCNY by then and again needed a summer job. I landed my summer job at Fotochrome because my brother Mike played in a band with a teenager, Paul, whose dad was a part owner of Fotochrome.

I worked for Fotochrome for two summers, 1961 and 62. I graduated with my degree in Electrical Engineering in January of 1963 and landed a full time job working for a company on Long Island known as Digital Electronics. Since I not longer needed summer work, I never worked in Manhattan again, and since it was no longer easy to get to Canal and Cortland Streets, I stopped going there. Also, since I was now developing sophisticated design skills, and also had some "real" money, I started purchasing parts for my various projects from places like Lafayette Radio and Allied Radio. I also bought stuff from a mail order business known as Herbach and Radiman.

I have many fond memories of my teenage years before getting married and spending time visiting the unique stores on both Canal and Cortland Streets. I can still picture the stores with the tables out front and the small groups of people like myself rummaging through boxes of interesting "stuff". I still have some of the "stuff" on the shelves of our basement and each time I run across something from the "good ole days" back in the 50's, I feel a tang of nostalgia and tears come to my eyes. Unfortunately, when the Twin Towers of the World Trade Center were built in the 1960's, the Port Authority of NY condemned Cortland Street, bought up all the stores on what was known as "Radio Row", and had the towers constructed. They were so expensive that they stood empty (for the most part) until the 1980's when the government in NY state started leasing space there. This was followed by many upscale companies following suit until most or all of the space was rented. My trip with REAP on the 25th also brought back these memories and prompted me writing this short story.

David and Goliath: The Modern Version

March 28, 2015

There is a well known biblical story about David who slays a giant Goliath by throwing stones at him with a slingshot. Goliath had been terrorizing David's people and David decides to challenge Goliath to put an end to his terrible deeds.

About four years ago, there is a similar story, a true one, that involved another kind of giant, the dutch based *Giant* food store chain, that decided to open one of their huge stores in the small town of Richboro, in lower Bucks County, Pennsylvania. The story is of personal interest, because my wife and I live in Churchville, just south of Richboro, and I was the "David" who decided to take on the Giant.

We moved to Churchville in 1967 about a year after leaving New York City where my wife and I were born, educated, married, had our first child, and then left for a more rural life in Bucks County, a suburb of Philadelphia. We were living in the home we purchased in 1967 for about 44 years when my bout with the Giant food chain started.

I was reading a local paper one day when an article appeared about Giant wanting to open one of their superstores right here in Richboro. Normally, this would not be of concern if it were not for several important factors. First, we already had three stores that my wife and I love to shop in for our food needs and all are located within two miles of where we live. Second, if a Giant were to open here in Richboro, it would most likely result in the closing of one and possibly two of the supermarkets that we already have and also impact the third, family run store, that sells mostly produce. This third store is located next to the farm that they own where they raise cattle and produce milk that they also sell in their store. We have been shopping at these three local stores for many years, have gotten to know the folks who work there, and enjoy our experiences shopping there.

When I read about Giant's wanting to open a store, a red flag went up. In addition to posing a threat to the existing three stores, it was clear, that our small town of Richboro, that has only one main street running through it, would be affected in a big way. The increase in the flow of cars and trucks would clearly raise the threat of more accidents involving both cars and pedestrians if the Giant were to open at the proposed location in Richboro.

Within a short time after reading about this article and the Giant wanting to come to Richboro, it was announced that our local township would be holding hearings to enable both the Giant to make a presentation to the public regarding their plans and to enable the citizens living here to respond and express their concerns.

I quickly decided that something had to be done to keep this new "Goliath" out of our town ship, so I started circulating a petition here in our own neighborhood to enable my neighbors to express their feelings. I also started working on a speech to deliver at the first public township meeting on the Giant's plans and how it would impact Richboro and the surrounding neighborhoods.

When the night came for the public meeting, I was the second one to speak. The list of concerned citizens was so long that the township had to schedule several meetings to enable everyone to express their concerns. At the first public hearing, Giant was given the opportunity to present its plans formally to the township in the presence of as many concerned citizens as wanted to attend the meeting. Originally, the meeting was to be held at the township building, but it was quickly decided that this venue would be too small, so the meeting was re-scheduled to take place in the auditorium of a local school.

The first meeting during which Giant presented its plans went smoothly enough however, during Giant's presentation, the supervisors had to silence the audience at several points when there were negative "outbursts" in response to some of the projections made by Giant. These projections many felt were way off base and unrealistic. Many of us felt that their consultants were paid to slant the presentation to make the proposed new store look more attractive and to downplay the impact its opening would have on traffic, noise, and lighting in the area.

At the second meeting that was opened to the public for their comments, I made my presentation that lasted about twenty minutes. At several points during my speech, people in the audience applauded. When I finished and was about to leave the microphone, virtually everyone in the audience stood up an applauded. The meeting went on until after mid-night and was followed a few weeks later by a second meeting to allow the remaining members of the public to speak. The day after I made my presentation, there was an article in the Bucks County Courrier Times, our local newspaper, that covered not only the meeting, but my presentation. I had also been interviewed after my presentation by a member of the newspaper who noted many of my comments.

As the plot unfolded over the next few months, I learned that our board of supervisors had been privately contacted by Giant and virtually all of the township supervisor board members were in favor of Giant's plans to open a supermarket in Richboro. Because of the public's response and to a large extent, my presentation, the supervisors had changed their positions and in the end decided unanimously against Giant. The bottom line was that Giant withdrew their plans and the whole thing just quietly "died". There were rumors in the months that followed that Giant had not really given up, but would try again in the future. I also said to my wife that although we had "won the battle", Giant would eventually try again in the future.

When I wrote this memoir in 2015, Giant had backed off and the three stores we shopped in continued to function. I would like to believe, that my efforts, in no small part, helped keep Richboro a small, friendly town, with safer streets, and helped the two existing supermarkets and a family owned store survive. Once again, a small "David" took on a formidable "Giant" and the "Giant" lost.

Note: It should be noted that when I reviewed this memoir for publication a Giant supermarket had taken over the space previously occupied by the "Shop-N-Bag" in Richboro and has been operating for about two years now. Murray, the previous owner retired. The good news is that the Giant did not open in the place previously planned but north of the originally planned location where there is plenty of off-the- street parking in a large lot in front of the store. Thus, my presentation several years ago was successful in that it prevented Giant from opening where it would have created a major traffic problem. In short, "David" won.

"Don't Sweat The Small stuff"

August 29, 2020

When I was a youngster, I heard many expressions used by the people in my life, including family, teachers and friends. Expressions like "Time Flies", "Don't Trust Anyone You Don't Like", and "Don't Sweat the Small Stuff". Over the years, I have come to appreciate expressions like "Time Flies", since it really does. Unfortunately, I have had several real life experiences that made me question the wisdom and validity of this last expression regarding the "Small Stuff".

Humans, and all creatures for that matter, often have to face the reality that all too often, we succumb to diseases and illness that take years off our lives. As an example, I lost a dear cousin to Hodgkin's Lymphoma at the early age of only 30. Cancer is caused by an abnormal multiplication of the bodies cells causing them to malfunction and also preventing surrounding cells to function normally. I, fortunately have not had to face cancer and hope I never do, however, on two occasions, I came close to losing my life due to insects that are very small and are all around us.

The first experience came when I was only forty years old and was cutting the lawn in our backyard. I was wearing sneakers and all of a sudden, I felt something sharp cut into my ankle. I instinctively hit the side of my sneaker with my fist, took off my sneaker and found a dying yellow jackets (wasp) in my sneaker. Not thinking much of this, I put my sneaker back on and continued cutting the lawn, when suddenly, I broke out into a sweat, started itching all over, and started feeling dizzy.

I ran into the house and reached for the bottle of liquid benedry that we fortunately had on the mantle of the fire place in our family room because one of our kids was having problems with exposure to the sun. I told my wife that I was stung and that I was having a reaction to the yellow jacket sting. She promptly called our doctor who told her to get me to the hospital ASAP and not to bother wasting the time to call an ambulance. The last thing I recall was grabbing the wall and lowering myself to the floor as I passed out.

My wife Judy and our kids managed to get me into a chair with casters, out the front door, and into the back of our Chevy station wagon. I don't recall the trip to St. Mary's Hospital in Langhorne, since I was in and out of consciousness. I do recall getting to the ER, and two nuns reaching toward me and putting a liquid, most likely ammonia, under my nose. This quickly got me up as they removed me from the wagon and put me into a wheel chair. I was immediately admitted and the doctor asked me what happened and what I did. I explained everything including taking the ounce or two of the benedryl. He said that there was nothing more to do so he put me on gluecose administered intravenously, and kept me on it for about an hour.

I was then discharged and went home.

I recall being "out of it" for about 24 hours. I recovered but was afraid to go outside for about a month. The good news is that I started seeing an immunologist who treated me with live yellow jacket venom to build up my immunity. It took about a year at which time I was declared immune, but had to keep an Epi-pen with me at all times. I was stung a few times after receiving the immunization treatment, but never had another reaction.

The latest incident occurred while my wife Judy and I were at our cabin in the Poconos. About four days after getting back from our cabin, my temperature suddenly shot up to about 103. I took aspirin and Tylenol that helped bring my temperature down, but after a few hours it climbed up again.

After about four days, I began to become dizzy and somewhat incoherent, so my wife called the medical facility in our retirement community and they immediately called an ambulance and I was brought to St. Mary's hospital once again. (but 40 years later). They had no idea what happened, but after leaving the ER and being transferred to a bed in a private room, I was immediately given antibiotics intravenously. Within 24 hours I had recovered to about 80% of normal. I was kept there for four days and was discharged with a bottle of Doxycycline pills, a strong antibiotic that I took for 6 days after leaving the hospital. Later in the week I was informed that I had been bitten by an infected tick and had a severe reaction to the tick bite. It was a very close call, but I recovered completely with no lingering effects.

In conclusion, when they say "Don't Sweat The Small Stuff", don't believe it. We are surrounded by insects in the warmer months (April to October) in the northeastern part of the USA, many of which can sting or bite. These include the wasp family, bees, mosquitoes and ticks. It makes good sense to consider insect repellents as well as pants and shirts that have been pretreated to repel dangerous insects. Also, when going outside, wearing long pants, socks, a long sleeve shirt, and a hat, can provide some protection. Of course, when it is very hot, wearing shorts and a short sleeve shirt can be more comfortable. Just don't forget, it is the small stuff that we have to be cautious of since it will generally be those that "get us" when we let our guard down.

"Drop Out, You'll Never Make It"

031920

I graduated from Evander Childs High School in the Bronx in June of 1958 and started on my bachelors degree in Electrical Engineering at CCNY, the City College of New York, that September. After registering for my fall classes, and impulsively signing up for a 2 year stint in the Army ROTC, (a mistake, but hey, we don't get everything right), I had to meet with an advisor who reviewed what I was registered for. My courses that fall were entirely in liberal arts since I was not due to start my engineering courses until two years later.

The advisor, a man who did not know me from the corner lamppost, after looking over my plans to pursue a degree in EE, looked up from his desk, stared me in the eyes and said very calmly: "Drop out, you'll never make it."

Over the next four and a half years, I worked very hard in persuing my dream to be an electronics engineer. I graduated in January of 1963 with a B average and started working for a small company located just off the Long Island Expressway in Westbury, long Island. While there I worked on one of the earliest digital general purpose computers that were being built for two of the cities community colleges. The computer as we know it today, did not exist, and the there was no monitor. An IBM Selectric typewriter was used as the input-output device and the memory was a rotating magnetic drum 4' X 2' by 2' that had an access and storage time of about 24 milliseconds. The storage capacity was about 6000 words of 18 bits per word. By today's standards it was in the ice age with respect to storage capacity and speed. It also used a Royal McBee paper tape reader punch to both input and store data. I also helped Grumman Aircraft in developing one of the earliest satellites called the OAO (Orbiting Astronomical Observatory). While at Digital Eelectronics from 63 to 65 I developed an interest in the field of SONAR, and left in Jan of 1965 to work in this field.

This continued until my wife and I decided to leave NY and move to Bucks County PA. This move was related to my interest in applying my skills and education in areas directly related to helping people rather than on military related endeavors. I landed a job with a small department of Norden, that was in Trevose for about 4 years from 1964 to 1968. The department was known as Telemedics and was doing pioneering work in the wireless transmission of the human EKG waveform to remote monitoring stations. I worked in this field for a year, when unexpectedily, the department was uprooted and moved to Connecticut.

I was left "high and dry", with a house under construction, when the shift occurred. I ended up shifting back to the Norden plant in Trevose and working on a sonar system that had already been designed and needed to be tested (debugged). This lasted for a year when I decided to move on and landed a job in Cheltenham working for a small independently owned company known as General

Atronics or GAC for short. I was there for 10 years and again had the opportunity to work on some very challenging programs.

While at GAC, I led the team that bid on and won a contract to develop the Voice Communication system for the NASA Space Shuttle. I also conceived of the concept behind the very popular interference canceling headsets. I worked on several different programs while at GAC, and was involved in developing some new and advanced types of digital encryption programs, to keep others from spying on our data and voice transmissions. Over time I had some new ideas related to highly efficient power conversion and regulation, and did some experimentation in the lab on these ideas. Unfortunately, GAC had neither the factilities or interest in letting me pursuing this work, so I decided to leave in the winter of 1978, and joined a medium sized company in Lansdale Pa, called the American Electronics Lab. (AEL) for short. AEL had the resources to support my work. While at AEL I landed a contract to help Boeing test the 757 and 767 aircraft that were being developed.

I left AEL and worked in the electrostatics field for thirteen years and designed and/or improved about forty devices for testing the properties of material when they become electrostatically charged.

My last job was in the special needs field when I worked for a non profit company called *The Woods School*". I was hired by the board of directors to start and manage a brand new department called "Assistive Technology". It involved the application of science and technology to help those with special needs live a more productive and happy life. I was there for eleven years and retired from this position in 2006. This last job was the most rewarding since I was helping people almost every day.

I wish I could meet the advisor who said "Drop out you'll never make it" and share my history.

Every Cloud Has a Silver Lining

As we go through life, we encounter difficulties that at the time seem very dark and grey. These are like a cloud that at times seems vast, and often very dark. As we gaze up at the sky, at these dark clouds, we ask: "Where will it end?" The dark clouds end, the sun comes out, and we see the silver lining.

During my life, there were these "dark clouds" (events), that often appeared, most often without warning, and at the time were devastating. As time passed however, the events ended and things got better.

The first event occurred when I was five years old and started kindergarten at P.S. 6 in the Bronx. I was a very difficult child, being curious and restless, and gave my teachers a very hard time, to put it mildly. By the time I entered the first grade, I had a title. It was: "The Holy Terror of P.S. 6". My reputation followed me into Junior High School, where, in the seventh grade, I was placed in the worst class. Fortunately, my grades were way above those of my classmates, so that I was placed in the second best class in the eighth and ninth grades. In high school, I made both the honor school, and senior arista. I also received an award at graduation for the highest level of achievement in physics.

A second event occurred when I was eighteen and an entering freshman enrolled in the Electrical Engineering Curriculum at CCNY. I had to meet with an advisor, who met with me to review what I had chosen as my major. After looking at the paperwork in my file, he looked up at me and said: "Drop out, you'll never make it." I paid little attention to what he had said, and continued with my plan to graduate with a degree. It took me four and a half years, the normal time to complete all of the necessary coursework, and I did succeed in getting my degree, however, there were many obstacles along the way, and at times, I was ready to quit. The advisor was correct in what he said since only about 10% of us enrolled in Electrical Engineering got our degrees out of about 1000 that enrolled at the start. Thus, this cloud had its silver lining since I went on to have a very successful career with several major accomplishments.

Another event occurred when I was working for an electronics laboratory in Lansdale, PA. I was the manager of a department with about 20 people. I took the job because the company had all the departments I needed, including a mechanical design group, a drafting department, and a transformer manufacturing department, to support the things I wanted to do. Unfortunately, the company kept "sidetracking" me by assigning me to other groups to solve their problems. This went on for three years, during which time, I never had the time to work on the things I wanted to work on. When the last assignment was successfully completed, and I had solved a major problem for another department, I sat in my office for two weeks, trying to figure out what to do next. My supervisor, called me into the office and asked me to resign from the company. I said, if you want to get rid of me, then you had better fire me. As a result I was immediately fired. This happened at a time when people my age were being let go and many had to start new careers. I felt that my career was over, and that I would never work as an electronics engineer again.

When I got home that afternoon, I called a friend who had been working for a small company in Glenside PA, and told him what had happened. He mentioned that his company shared the loft they were in with a tiny company (two employees) and that they needed help. I called the company and was asked if I could stop in and help them solve a problem with a major piece of test equipment that was not working. I made the trip to Glenside from Churchville and immediately solved the problem. It was related to radiation that was causing the equipment of malfunction. I was hired on the spot to serve as an independent consultant to help them design and build new test equipment. Fortunately, before leaving the company in Lansdale, PA, I had started my own consulting company called Noran Technical Consultants, so getting started was very simple. I continued working for this company as a consultant for four years. I did most of the design work at home since I had assembled a small electronics work area many years before, and had everything in place to do design, breadboarding and testing of electronic circuits, which was my specialty. A friend I had met many years earlier did the printed board layout work. Again, what started out as a dark cloud, ended up with a silver lining.

I eventually joined this small company and handled all of the electronic design work. I also got involved in the marketing and sales efforts. I was with this company for nine more years as a full time employee, but it ended on a sour note when I was fired because of conflicts I had with the president of the company.

Again, I thought my working career was over, but a few months later, landed a new job working for a company that provided services for folks of all ages with special needs. I was hired to start a brand new department called "AssistiveTechnology". Over the next eleven years, I worked independently as the manager of this department doing all the client evaluations and the design or modification of devices to help those with special needs. Over the eleven years that I worked there, I helped enrich the lives of about twenty thousand people. It was the best job I ever had.

In summary, when things look bad and there is no hope in sight, the "dark cloud" often has a bright (silver) lining. Things generally get better, and often are actually better than before the "disaster" struck.

Finding Blue Roof

8/24/12

It was the summer of 1985 and my wife Judy and I were vacationing in Ontario Canada and were winding down our two week vacation. We had spent the past week and a half touring Montreal and Ottawa and were wandering southwest from Ottawa toward what was known as "the lakes region".

We were heading south toward Kingston, Just above the St. Lawrence River and needed a place to stay for the night. On this particular trip we were kind of "winging it" and had not made specific plans on where to stay each night. We stumbled on a small town called Verona where we had lunch and spent some time wandering in and out of the small shops in town. In one of the shops we found a brochure describing a farm outside of town that was being run as something called a "Bed and Breakfast. We drove out to the farm and found that they had one room left, so we took it. We had never stayed at a "B & B" before, so were excited about this new experience.

After signing the guest register we took our two small suitcases to our room and were very pleased to find that it was much nicer than most of the motels we had stayed at in the past. It was furnished with primarily antique furniture, a beautiful vintage mirror, and all sorts of cute little things that one just does not find in a typical motel or hotel room. The only negative I can recall was that we had to share the one bathroom with the other guests who were also spending the night at the same B & B. This turned out to be a minimal issue.

Our hosts turned out to be very nice people who quickly gave us guidance on where to have dinner in Verona that night. We took their recommendation and had a nice reasonably price meal in the center of town. The following morning, we had a nice breakfast at the farm which was prepared by our hosts using eggs from their own chickens. We had breakfast with the other folks who were also guests and quickly decided that B & B's were the way to go in the future. Motels and hotels are nice, but very impersonal. We liked the idea of meeting new people and having friendly discussions both in the evenings and/or at breakfast.

Before leaving, we spent some time thanking our hosts for the great experience we had had at their farm. Our hosts mentioned that they had a friend nearby who had just started a B & B that was called Blue Roof and that the owner was a woman named Kim. Before leaving, they gave us directions on how to get to Blue Roof and a new brochure with directions and a description of this nice sounding place.

We drove back to Verona, walked through the quaint little town and found a neat little shoe store that sold name brand shoes at discounted prices. My wife found several pairs of shoes that we purchased, returned to our car, and remembered the brochure we were given by our B & B hosts.

I found the brochure, and began to read the directions. It said to take a left on a small paved road just south of Verona, travel about ¾ of a mile down the road until coming to a cross road where there was an old abandoned grist mill and to take a right on the smaller road at the mill. It said to continue until passing a small farm with some cows grazing in a field on the left. It continued: "Watch for a white picket fence on the right with a pond surrounded by flowers, and a small house with a bright blue metal roof, to look for an opening in the fence and a driveway on the right with a big wagon wheel and to turn into the driveway." It also said not to be surprised if we were greeted by "Gus the Goose" wobbling toward us in the driveway, and "Casey the Cat" sitting on the fence, and not to be alarmed if two friendly Dalmatians come running toward us as we approach the house. Since we had no plans for the afternoon, and had no plans for where to stay for the night, we decided to check out this very nice sounding thing called "Blue Roof". I started the car and headed south out of Verona.

In a few minutes we came to a smaller road and turned right continuing for about ¾ of a mile until we came to the small grist mill. At the mill, we took another right as noted in the brochure and continued until we came to a farm with cows grazing in a field to our right. This was followed by a white picket fence and then we saw the small house with a bright blue roof, the pond in front, surrounded with trees and beautiful flowers between the house and fence. As in the brochure, we took a left when there was an opening in the fence with two big white wagon wheels, one on each side of the fence.

I slowly inched down the short dirt driveway, parked the car and my wife Judy and I got out and started walking toward the house with the bright blue roof. Within a few seconds, I noticed a white goose ("Gus?") waddling down the driveway toward us, and there on the left, perched on the fence, was a black and white cat ("Casey?"). As we continued walking toward the house, there suddenly appeared two black and white large Dalmatians! I abruptly stopped and turned to my wife and said: "Hey, this is impossible, things like this only happen in Disneyland!"

We walked up to the front porch of Blue Roof and were greeted by a teenaged girl who welcomed us and offered us some lemonade. She said that Kim, the owner of Blue Roof had gone to Kingston to do some shopping and would be back shortly. In a few minutes, a car drove up and we met Kim Ondatje, who sat down with us on the porch to sip some lemonade. She told us about Blue Roof and how she and her former husband Michael had started Blue Roof as a farm to raise organic cattle and how they had checked the past history of the property to ensure that chemicals had never been used to spray anything that had been grown on the farm. They raised a herd of cattle that were sold periodically for the organically grown beef. She started to run Blue Roof as a B & B because the farmer who helped with the herd, had medical problems and could no longer help with the care of the cattle. she gave us a tour of the house and told us about the swimming area that was about ½ mile down a narrow dirt road that led to the secluded pond. Kim told us that the road traveled through a beautiful open meadow with numerous wildflowers and scattered with some trees. We asked if we could visit the swimming area, and she said yes. She then turned to one of the Dalmatians and quietly told him to accompany us to the swimming area and make sure we didn't get lost. We watched in amazement as this rather large dog seemed to gaze intently at her and appeared to be listening carefully. We opened the gate to meadow, and proceeded to walk toward the pond that was hidden in some trees at the far end of the meadow. The Dalmatian that Kim had spoken to, promptly got up and walked ahead of us down the path leading to the meadow. We strolled leisurely down the narrow dirt path in the meadow and frequently stopped to look at the beautiful wildflowers that were blooming all over the place. The Dalmatian would stop and wait patiently for us to finish, and then would continue with us. He would run ahead of us on the path, then stop and wait for us to catch up before running ahead again. This routine continued till we reached the pond.

The pond was hidden in the trees, and would be impossible to find if one did not know it was there. It was located down the end of a small path that led through the woods. The setting surrounding the pond was very serene and the pond itself was simply out of a fairy tale. We quickly named this spot "The Blue Lagoon". We sat on the warm sand gazing at the beautiful pond and the wonderful setting while the Dalmatian patiently sat near us. When we got up to leave and return to the house, he promptly got up and let us back through the meadow to the gate next to the house. As soon as we reached the gate next to the house, he took one more look at us and, knowing we were safely back, ran off.

Judy and I quickly decided that we would love to spend some time at Blue Roof, so we asked Kim if we could spend the night. She apologized and told us that she was full for that night and could not accommodate us that night or the next, but after a few minutes of thought said that she wanted us to experience a day at Blue Roof and offered us her own suite for the night. She told us that she would sleep in the "chicken coop". We immediately refused indicating that we could not displace her to sleep in a chicken coop. She explained that it wasn't really a chicken coop, but one that had been converted to a small one room cabin that was very comfortable but did not have a bathroom. She indicated that she would come into the main house if she needed to use the bathroom at night. We then agreed to spend the night there, stay for breakfast, and possibly take a swim in the afternoon before leaving for our return trip home.

We unpacked our suitcase, and since it was a warm afternoon, decided to get into our bathing suits, take a stroll through the beautiful meadow again, and take a swim in the pond that we had visited earlier. We spent about an hour at "The Blue Lagoon" just swimming and enjoying the clear cool water and the beautiful surroundings. Of course, Kim had one of Dalmatians accompany us again, to make sure that we were OK and didn't get lost. While we swam, he just sat in the shade waiting for us to finish.

Kim's living area at Blue Roof was just incredible. It had a king sized bed in the bedroom next to which was a heated Jacouzzi. It was all finished in knotty pine and had a kitchen and dining room next to the bedroom. There was a large picture window in the dining room overlooking a pasture with cows grazing there. The whole place was simply idyllic.

We slept well that night and Kim prepared a great breakfast the following morning. After breakfast, we spent some time getting to know Kim and learn more about Blue Roof and how she happened to end up there.

We spent a total of two days there on our first visit, but returned at least four more times until about 1990 the year after we purchased our cabin in the Poconos. We maintained contact with Kim for several years, but gradually drifted apart, since there was no longer the need to drive to Canada to get away for a vacation. We also discontinued our trips to Maine to vacation in Rangely since the Poconos had trees, streams, lakes and woods similar to Maine.

Finding Blue Roof was a significant milestone in our lives since we discovered the B & B way of traveling, made a new friend, and had several summers of fun taking walks in a pristine environment, swimming in its unique swimming hole, meeting many interesting new people who were also guests at Blue Roof, and just relaxing. It is now over 30 years since our first contact with Kim and Blue Roof. I believe it is still there and Kim is there also. Perhaps its time for a letter or phone call and perhaps another trek up north to rekindle an old friendship.

Note: Kim, whose last name is Ondatje, it turned out, had been married to Michael Ondatje, the man who wrote the book "The English Patient" on which the movie was based. This movie won an academy award in 1992 for the best screenplay.

Flashback To The Big Band Era

16/20/2016

This story takes place in los angeles in the 1970's while I was on a business trip and spent the better part of a week on the west coast.

I was working for a company called Genral Atronics Corp. (gac) located on mermaid lane in Cheltenham, PA. And had landed a navy contract to develop encryption software so that information could be transmitted from one place to another without others receiving these transmissions and listening in to the conversations, or downloading and using the transmitted data.

As it turned out, the navy had also awarded a contract to Hughes Aircraft (hac) in Culver City, CA to develop ways of using integrated circuit technology to reduce the size, weight and cost of building and producing complex systems. Even though Hughes Aircraft was much larger than gac, the navy made us the prime and hac, the subcontractor to us. Since I had managed the writing of the proposal for this contract, I was chosen by gac to manage and lead the design team on this program. The prime objective was to develop encryption software and build systems with this encryption using the Hughes integrated circuit technology.

One difficulty I encountered on this program was the fact that Hughes was on the west coast, and gac was on the east coast and I quickly learned that the hughe team was not interested in coming east when we had to hold our regular program review meetings. As a result, about 90% of the time, I had to travel to la to hold our regular meetings.

I usually brought with me, my design team, and when we met with Hughes, they had their support team as well, which usually included their contracts administrator. This tall gentleman, who at the time was in his sixties, had a deep resonant voice and was somewhat distinguished looking. We usually spent the day covering the status of the program, any technical difficulties, and how the costs were going. After concluding our meetings, usually late in the afternoon, we usually went to dinner somewhere in the la area.

One evening, after we had concluded our meeting of the day, we went to dinner at a nice restaurant in la and since the night was still young, we started contemplating what to do after dinner. At this point, the Hughes contracts administrator, suggested we shift over to a piano bar in the san fernando valley, where we could have a few drinks and engage in a lively discussion. He indicated that he had been there several times and that at about 9pm a guy who played the piano usually showed up and we could enjoy his playing. We agreed that this was a good plan, so we hopped into our cars, got onto rt 101, otherwise known as the san diego freeway, and headed north through the beverly hills to the valley.

We reconvened at the small lounge, ordered a few drinks and just hung out till about 9pm, when a short guy appeared, sat down at the piano, and started playing. After a few songs, the Hughes contracts administrator, got up, slowly went over to the piano, noded to the piano player, and started singing along to the tune he had been playing. As I listened, my mouth dropped when I heard his voice. He was nothing short of a knock out! He knew the words and melody of every song he sang.

After singing a few songs, the contracts administrator, just sat down and started sipping his unfinished drink. I slowly turned to him and said: "where did you learn to sing like that?" His answer floored me when he said: "in the 1940's, I was the lead singer for "The Modernares" and sang with the big bands inculding the Dorsey brothers, Tommy and Jimmy".

It is interesting to note that you never know who you may run into in your travels. In this case, my chance meeting with this guy from hughes aircraft, while running a high tech program, led me back to the big band era and I had a chance to mingle with someone who sang with two of my favorite big bands from that historic time in america.

Flashback to the Civil Rights Movement

Feb 25, 2013 rev 1

In June of 2005, I was attending a RESNA* Assistive Technology Conference in Atlanta and was staying at the hotel in downtown Atlanta where the three–day conference was being held. My wife Judy accompanied me to the conference and spent the days touring Atlanta while I attended the presentations and exhibits at the conference.

One of the high points of the trip was during a break I took from the conference to take a guided tour of the restored Fox Theater on Peachtree Street not too far from our hotel. I am a lover of organ music, and was thrilled when my wife and I had a chance to attend a lecture conducted by the organist of the 4,000 pipe, Mighty Möller theater organ, Larry-Douglass Embury, as part of the tour. This theater is a real gem and a must see in Atlanta.

When the conference ended, we had another treat when we learned that the Atlanta Symphony Orchestra gives free concerts during the summer season in Piedmont Park. We borrowed a blanket from the hotel, took the train a few stops north, and walked a few blocks to the park. It was great listening to a terrific orchestra play many familiar tunes while sitting on our blanket under a tree. I recall meeting a nice couple next to us who had brought a picnic dinner and shared some wine with us.

After the concert, we took the train back to our hotel. Even though it was about 10PM and dark, the city was still very hot and humid, and the thought of a nice cold strawberry thick shake sounded very good. Remembering that there was a McDonald's just around the corner from our hotel, we headed there for refreshing break before heading back to our room.

Unfortunately, when we arrived at the McDonald's, it looked like everyone in Atlanta had the same idea. There were two long lines of people, probably about 15 deep, also waiting to get some treats and a cold drink. Since we had nothing else to do that evening, we decided to wait for our turn at the counter and two cold thick shakes.

We noticed that standing in the line to our right was a distinguished looking elderly gentleman dressed in a three piece suit, tie and a brimmed hat. He was an African American and his trim white hair and beard stood out nicely against his dark skin color.

We struck up a conversation with this fine looking man and after some small talk (our being in Atlanta for the convention, the concert that we had just attended, and the fact that we were heading home for Pennsylvania in the morning), he mentioned that he was originally from Birmingham Alabama, and that they had erected a statue of him in front of the library in Birmingham. He said that he was involved in the Civil Rights Movement and had marched with Martin

Luthor King in the early 1960's, but no longer lived in Birmingham. He also mentioned that he was the pastor of his own church. Since we didn't know this man from Adam, my wife and I looked at each other with a puzzled look and didn't know what to make of what he had said. Quite frankly, we both felt he was most likely just an old geezer who had probably lost some of his marbles.

By now, the lines were shrinking and we were both approaching the counter, and knew that we would soon part, so we shook hands and bid each other farewell before we parted. The last thing he said to us was that his name was Fred Shuttlesworth.

We returned from the Atlanta the next day, but our meeting with this distinguished gentleman at McDonald's was still haunting us, so my wife Judy, decided to do some research on the internet and found out that there was minister by the name of Fred Shuttlesworth who did participate in the civil rights movement, did march with Martin Luthor King, and that there was a statue of him in Birmingham. What a surprise!

It is now 6 years later, October 6 of 2011 to be specific. It was the day after the death of Steve Jobs, the mover and shaker of Apple Computer, and I was reading the Philadelphia Inquirer newspaper and happened to turn to the obituary section where there was an extensive article on Steve Jobs, covering his life and career. To my surprise and shock, there, on the same page, was an obituary on a distinguished gentleman who died that same day. His name was Fred Shuttlesworth.

Life is very interesting and unpredictable, and one never knows who you may run into and under what circumstances. What I have learned however, is that no matter what the situation, it pays to take a little time out of your busy life to be kind, considerate and congenial no matter what the time, place or circumstances. When you meet someone new, whether on vacation, in the supermarket, at the theater, or anyplace for that matter, take the time to get to know the folks around you. You may look back someday and find that you have met some very interesting and sometimes very prominent people. And they have not only made a difference in your life, but perhaps you have made a difference in theirs as well.

*RESNA- Rehabilitation Engineering Society of North America

Bound for Birmingham Jail on Good Friday 1963 are
(from left) the Revs. Fred Shuttlesworth, Ralph Abernathy,
and Martin Luther King Jr.   Birmingham, Ala., Public Library Archives

Statue of Fred Shuttlesworth
Civil Rights Institute, Birmingham,
Ala.

"Forgive and Forget": Often easier to say than do!"

❦

February 22, 2014

When I was a young boy growing up in the Bronx, I would listen to the growups talk and would often hear them use what were known as clichés, one of which was phrase that when someone says or does something that you do not like to just "forgive and forget". I also discovered that my grandmother, who often used these clichés, had a falling out with her own sister, and had not spoken to her in twenty five years. This was a "puzzlement" to me since she could not practice what she preached (i.e. "forgive and forget").

Also, as a child, and even as a younger adult, I believed that in most families, there was harmony and a sense of "togetherness" that made for a happy family environment. I really believed that this was the "norm" in the world. As I went through life both in my profession, and personally, I had the opportunity to meet and get to know people from all over the world and to talk to them about their relationships with those around them. Over time, and little by little, my "take" on how things were, began to change. I found for example, that it is very common for one family member to isolate themselves from another family member for great lengths of time. I discovered that this happened between brothers and sisters and sometimes (unfortunately) even between a parent and one or more of his or her children. I even learned as I grew older, that even in my own immediate family, there were bad feelings between many of my cousins and aunts and uncles that I was oblivious to as a child. I learned that things just happened that created gaps in relationships, and that these gaps often developed into gaping holes. This became very personal since I too was to "lose" a brother and sister because of acts of selfishness and inconsideration, that occurred repeatedly and over a long period of time that forced me, as a means of protecting me, my wife and my children, from harm.

I do believe that one should be tolerant of others and try to not focus on the small stuff, but when the "small stuff" becomes "big stuff" and repeatedly, causes harm, usually psychological, one has to adopt practices to protect oneself from this kind of damage. In my case, with respect to my brother, I also personally suffered physical damage when, during the course of what was a civil discussion, triggered rage in my brother, and cause me to suffer two broken ribs.

Psychological damage was also caused by my own sister that over close to thirty years finally resulted in my "crossing her off my list". When these things happen one is forced not to forget so as to prevent further damage. Also, forgiving becomes difficult if not impossible. In short, the term "forgive and forget", may sound like good advice, but in real life, it is often difficult if not impossible to do. Fortunately, my wife and I have very good relationships with her two sisters and their families and we have never had to think about forgiving and forgetting.

Fragile Friendships

020421

A few years after we are born, we begin to connect with people outside of our immediate family. We call these people "friends", and as we progress along this path we call life, we make friends with many people, but as we will learn, these friendships are fragile, and, in an instant, can come to an end.

Our first friends are usually in our own neighborhood, but when we start nursery school, at about the age of two to five, we start to connect with other youngsters and they quickly become our friends. When we start going to kindergarten, we make more friends, and our nursery friendships, may or may not continue.

If we are lucky, and our parents don't move to another neighborhood, we will continue to progress upward in grade school, and at each grade level, we add new friends. We then progress to middle school and make new friends that we meet in our classes. After this we progress to high school and again, are introduced to additional new friends. When I entered Evander Childs HS, in the Bronx, I met a fourteen year old girl who was to become my lifelong "friend". Her name was Judy, and little did I know at the time, she would be with me for the rest of my life since we married seven years later and are still together as I write this.

When I graduated Junior High School, many of my friends joined me and attended Evander High School, but many went on to other high schools and our friendships ended. After this, it was college, and I started on my engineering degree at CCNY, the City College of New York. This was a major step since most of those who I attended high school with did not attend CCNY but started working and never went to college. But as before, I met a whole new group of college friends who "traveled" with me at CCNY for the next four and a half years.

When I graduated, I started my graduate work in the evening and attended New York University. Here again, a new group of friends. I also started working in my chosen profession at a small company called Digital Electronics in Westbury Long Island. Again, new people entered my life at Digital. This was followed by two job changes onr in Lake Success and one in College Point where I worked in the sonar field. After three and a half years, my wife and I decided to relocate to Bucks County, PA and started a new life with our daughter Joy, who was 2 ½ years old. Again, a whole new group of friends both at work and where we lived, first in Trevose, and then in Churchville, after our new home was finished.

During the next forty years, there were eight more job changes and more people I worked with many of which became friends. My wife, taught at a local middle school, and again, more friends.

Perhaps the greatest number of friends I made on any one job was the one I retired from. It was in Langhorne where I worked for a non-profit company called the Woods School. I started and was the manager of the Assistive Technology Department and met new folks, both clients and staff. I retired at the normal retirement age, and went out "with a bang" since a surprise party was thrown for me by the people I worked with. About four years later I joined a group called REAP (Retired Executives and Professionals) and almost instantly, about seventy new people entered my life. I also joined a local senior center and made friends with over twenty new seniors.

My wife and I decided to leave our home and enter an over 65 community called Pennswood Village, where again, we connected with retired folks from all over the world, many of whom became new friends.

In summary, as one travel through life we meet people, and make many friends. I guess it is normal for these friendships to be fragile since we often change the neighborhoods we live in, the companies we work for, and in many cases the places where we live. With each change, we leave some friendships behind, and we make new ones after the change. Such is life. Few of us carry with us the friendships we make along the way. I am not happy with this, but this is the way it is. Friendships are simply fragile.

Gardening: My Favorite Hobby

—— ❧ ——

I like gardening because I believe it is a great hobby. Although I have and had many leisure time activities that include photography, woodworking, reading, model railroading, electronic design, landscape painting and inventing new things, gardening is my favorite.

I have always been fascinated by nature and living things and perhaps enjoy gardening so much because it enables me to get very close to "mother earth" and take an active part in helping make things grow and making the world of ours greener and more beautiful.

I was born in New York City and lived in an apartment building in the city, and was unable to become involved in gardening until the age of 12 when my parents bought a small semi-attached (duplex) home in the north eastern section of the Bronx just a few blocks from the city line. Our new home had a small backyard and, in the spring of 1952, my dad bought some garden tools and I planted my first home garden that included both vegetables and a few annual flowers.

After leaving the Bronx in 1966 I lived with my family in our own home in Northamptown Township, Bucks County on a 1/2 acre lot. There was ample room for me to engage in a variety of gardening activities including vegetable and flower gardening as well as landscape design.

My grandfather, who immigrated to the US from Russia in 1905, was the one who most likely first kindled my interest in gardening when I was still a young boy. After living in Brooklyn, NY for several years, he bought a small farm in Liberty NY and moved there with his family. In the late 1940's, while I was still living with my parents in our small apartment, my dad would make the 100 mile trip from the Bronx to Liberty once or twice each year, so that our family could visit with my grandparents who had retired to a small home about half a mile from Liberty. I loved my grandparents very much and looked forward our visits with them. When we visited in the summer or early fall, my grandfather would take me into his small vegetable garden and together we would pick carrots, beets, and string beans, or whatever was ready for harvesting. I can still recall the rich dark soil and lush, green plants in his garden, as well as the wonderful experience of eating the freshly picked vegetables that my grandmother would cook and serve with dinner.

Although the basics of gardening have not changed over the years (we still work with soil, light, water and air) many new things are available now that did not exist when I started gardening over 50 years ago. Today there are many more varieties that are readily available to the average gardener in the form of seeds, started plants, shrubs and trees, bulbs and perennials. Also, many improvements have been made in materials that help plants grow better (fertilizers) and help plants survive the attacks of bugs, insects and plant diseases. Advances have also been made in the tools and techniques that we use today. Drip irrigation is one example of a watering technique that was relatively unknown when I started gardening, but is used by many gardeners today. It is method of delivering water very slowly, literally a drop at a time through a specially designed hose system, that conserves water while delivering water to a plant's root system where it is most needed.

In the mid 1980's I combined my interest in gardening with my constant striving to make things better and easier, and designed a completely new kind of hand tool that I named "Wonder Weeder". This single small hand tool enables a gardener to weed, cultivate, plant, mix in soil additives, make furrows and maintain a flower bed edge. In my small way, I believe I had advanced the art of gardening through the introduction of my new invention, the "Wonder Weeder".

Perhaps the most important thing I learned from gardening is that everything in life has a cycle. Things are born and grow and, just like young children, who need care and nurturing, plants must also be cared for if they are to reach maturity. Later in the life cycle, as fall approaches, virtually all plants take steps to ensure the continuation of their kind by producing seeds. Then as winter approaches, their life cycle winds down. In the spring, seeds germinate, and new plants begin to grow as the cycle of life continues.

Today, my wife and I live in a retirement community not too far from where we lived in Churchville. I have a 650 square foot garden in the community garden. It enables me to continue gardening and raising both vegetables and flowers. We harvest mostly beets, tomatoes and peppers, but about 80% of the plot is flowers consisting of zinnias, marigolds, dahlias, ageratum and celosia. Even in my retirement years, I am happy to still be enjoying gardening.

How We met "Dr. Kildare" While Touring the Hawaiian Islands

It is interesting to look back during ones travels through life and reflect on the unusual places you visited and people you have met. One interesting experience (of many) that comes to mind is when my wife and I accidentally met Richard Chamberlain, who was probably best known for the TV mini-series *The Thorn Birds* and his role in the highly popular TV weekly program in the 1960's known as *Dr. Kildare.*

It was April of 1984 and my wife Judy and I decided to make our first pilgrimage to the Hawaiian Islands. It was a two week visit that started on the Big Island and ended when we returned to Honalulu for our return flight to Philadelphia. On this trip we managed to visit four Hawaiian Islands; the big island of Hawaii, Maui, Kawaii and Oahau. We stayed primarily in motels and hotels as part of a package deal on each island that enabled us to have a car, a place to stay and generally included breakfast. If my memory is correct the average price we paid per day for this great package was about fifty dollars. I challenge anyone to come even close to this today!

We spent about 4 days on each island and pretty much covered everything that there was to see and do on each one with the exception of Oahau. Since this was the most "touristy" island, we decided to spend only our last day there and just see the main sights in Honalulu like the Arizona Memorial, and the big shopping mall downtown.

During the first part of our visit we were touring the most southern island, the "Big Island", better known as Hawaii. On this particular day we were staying in Hilo and decided to drive up to the famous (still active) Haliakala Crater and see the sights from the single road that covers the rim of the crater. We were nearing the end of our drive and were on the western part of the crater when we pulled into a parking lot and immediately noticed a large white limousine with dark tinted windows parked there when we arrived. Since we were enchanted with the spectacular views we had experienced while traveling around the crater, and were much more interested in visiting this last overlook of the crater, we didn't think much of the white limo, so we parked our car and proceeded to walk down the stone path that led to the overlook of the crater.

The narrow, but mostly level path led to a small overlook with a wooden railing. Beyond the railing was an abrupt drop-off that fell to the floor of the crater several hundred feet below us. It was somewhat scary since this flimsy railing was the only thing separating us from the overlook and the floor of the crater. From this vantage point, we could see hot spots of lava with sulphur-laden fumes rising upward. I had my 35mm Minolta SRT 102 with several lenses with me, so I quickly started snapping off shots of the spectacular views of the crater.

I continued taking pictures from this vantage point when suddenly, I felt someone poke me in the ribs. It was my wife Judy, and she had a look of astonishment on her face and was pointing directly to our left. I turned my head to the left and to my amazement, there, no more than three feet away, was Richard Chamberlain and a companion leaning on the railing and looking into the crater. Without thinking much, I slowly walked up the path away from the railing, changed to my 200 mm adjustable zoom lens, raised my camera and snapped a great shot of Judy facing this famous star just as he turned to face her.

Judy and I then returned to our car and I recall saying to a couple that had just arrived; "Dr. Kildare is down the path looking at the crater". We got into our car and then returned to Hilo. Our chance meeting this celebrity at the crater turned out to be one of the most lasting memories of this great trip. Of course, we had other interesting experiences on this same visit to the Hawaiian Islands, but these are for another time.

End

How I "Skipped" 9ᵀʰ Grade Science

When I entered the eighth grade at Olinville Junior High School (P.S. 113) in the Bronx, New York, in 1954, my home room was switched from class 7-11, the lowest level class in the seventh grade to 8-2, the second highest for that grade. The reason I ended up in 7-11 was because of the poor record I entered JHS with from my past years in grade school. While attending grade school at P.S. 6 from 1945 until 1952, I was known as "the holy terror or PS 6" but that is for another story.

In either case, my home room class in the 8ᵗʰ and 9ᵗʰ grades was also a science class room with the usual experiment sink and granite counter top in the front of the room. My teachers name was Mrs. Rand for home room and it turned out, also for science in the 9ᵗʰ grade.

On my first day in science class in the ninth grade, I looked over the science coursework schedule for the year and quickly realized that I already knew most of the subject matter that I was scheduled to learn that year. Of more importance was that in the corner of the science room was a glass encased photographic dark room that was there but was unused. This is significant, because at about the age of 12, I had developed an interest in photography and at home, was developing rolls of size 120 black and white film and making contact prints since I did not have an enlarger. I was excited about discovering this fully equipped dark room in the corner of my science room that included an enlarger.

After a few days of thought about this darkroom in my science class just sitting there doing basically nothing, it occurred to me that my time could be better spent in the darkroom making enlarged prints, than in the science class being bored, since I already knew most of the material that was to be covered.

As a result, I decided to approach my teacher, and ask her if she would give me permission to work in the dark room in the science classroom instead of sitting through the science lessons. My friend Ben, who was in my science class, had already agreed to give me a copy of his handwritten classroom science notes that I agreed to type up and give him a copy of. I explained to my teacher that I would learn all of the lessons from typing up Ben's notes, take all of her science tests with my class and be fully responsible for passing them. Since she knew me well and knew that I would do well in science, she agreed to allow me to work in the darkroom instead of sitting through her science lessons.

The bottom line is that I basically "skipped" science in the ninth grade, had fun and learned about black and white enlarging and printing during the science lesson period in JHS, but still passed ninth grade science with flying colors. My friend Ben, also did well, since he had my clearly typed science notes to learn from. This was clearly an example of a win-win-win situation. The school won since I put an idle room to use, Ben won since he got a great grade in science that year, and I won twice, since I both learned a great deal about photofinishing and also passed science with a great grade.

How Much Is "Free" Going To Cost Me?

10/20/20

Over the years, I have been plagued by phone calls, pop-up surveys, and mailings from companies offering stuff for free. I have on several occasions taken the time to respond by answering numerous questions and then being offered a so called free gift as a reward for responding to each survey. In almost every case, there was a catch. Typically, the free gift requires the payment of a fee, usually listed as shipping and handling. In too many cases, the fee is not necessarily small, and in some cases, there are hidden clauses that require you to sign up for a membership with a recurring monthly fee. In at least two recent cases, the so called "free" gift, which cost me about $9 (for shipping and handling), turned out to be a trial of the gift for which I was later billed close to $100. On looking into it further, I discovered that one of the free gifts could have been purchased for about $25.

My earliest recollection of something offered for "free", came over the phone and was from a youngster who was hired by a major record and CD company to offer free gifts. The opener was: "Would I like 6 CD's for free"? I immediately said: "Yes, just send them to me." I was then told that I would have to pick the free CD's from an extensive list. I chose classical music as the genre, but discovered that I already had the ones being offered. The young girl said, they were free, so why don't I just choose 6 anyway. I then proceed to select 6 nice classical selections, hoping to end the call and get my 6 free CD's. I was then asked to provide a credit card number. Surprised, I asked why? I was told that there was a "small" shipping charge for my free CD's. But I said that I was told that they were free. The girls said that they were, but that the company had to charge for shipping them to me. I then asked how much the free CD's were and she said only $3.95 each! Using "advanced calculus" (joke), I arrived at a grand total of about $24 for my "free" CD's. I politely reminded the girl that if they were free, there should be no charge at all, but she just repeated that they were free. I was getting annoyed at this point so I suggested that the girl get a copy of a Webster's dictionary and look up the word "free". I suggested that to the best of my recollection, free meant "at no cost". Since the cost would be about $24, they were not free. She reiterated her line about shipping and handling, so I told her to offer someone else the "free" CD's (for $24) and I promptly hung up. I estimate that I had wasted at least fifteen minutes on the phone with her.

My most recent example of what free means, came when I agreed to respond to an on-line survey. The questions were numerous and the survey took about 10 minutes to complete. After the survey I was told that I could select a "free" gift for taking the time to do the survey. Three of the gifts were supplements to boost libido, but the fourth was a nice digital watch. I then selected the watch and was then asked for my credit card to cover just shipping and handling. The cost was supposed to be $6.95. I filled out the required fields with my credit card information and clicked done. About a week later a very nice watch showed up in the mail and I began to wear it. About three weeks later, I received my credit card statement and went into shock when I found that I had been billed $98 for the watch in addition to the $6.95 that I thought was the full cost. I promptly called the company and discovered that buried in the small print at the bottom of the offer were two items that were overlooked by me. One was that the watch was offered on a 16 day trial for the cost of $6.95 after which, if I decided to keep it, I would be billed the full price of $98. I also discovered that I had agreed to sign up for their monthly membership with a cost of $20 per month. I promptly got a supervisor on the phone, and told her that I was enraged by what they had pulled and that I intended to take action by reporting them to the Better Business Bureau as well as the federal government for fraud. I told her that I was a senior and had a severe vision issue and that what they had done was clearly deceptive. She seemed sympathetic and unlike the initial person I spoke to on this matter, said that I could keep the watch for the $6.95 I had paid and that they would not charge me any additional fees. She also agreed to drop the requirement that I join their monthly membership club for future offers. Fortunately this ended the matter, and all additional costs were credited back to card.

I had a second experience only recently with a major discount department store, again involving a short survey and a so called "free" gift. After completing the survey, I was promised a free virtual reality headset, something that I had heard about and wanted to check out. Again, the cost was supposed to be for shipping and handling only and amounted to $8.95. This time, after completing my selection, and providing my credit card info, I decided to go back and read the small print. Here again, I discovered that it was a trial only and required that after trying the headset, I could keep it if I paid the full price of about $100.

Again, this was "dirty pool" so I promptly called the company and they agreed to cancel everything. I told them to not send me anything, and also said as politely as I could to shove the headset you know where.

The bottom line is that we live in America that is "The Land Of Opportunity". Unfortunately, there are numerous companies out there who are looking to take advantage of unsuspecting people, many of whom are not youngsters, and sell them stuff under the guise of being "free" when in fact this stuff is anything but free. Yes, this is "The Land Of Opportunity", but unfortunately, we, the consumers, represent the opportunity for the millions of companies who want to sell whatever goods and or services they offer.

If someone contacts you and offers you something for free, simply ask: "What is free going to cost me?"

How A Webbcore Phonograph Changed My Life

When I was 15 years old and lived on Murdock Avenue in the Bronx (New York City) with my parents, my dad surprised me and bought me a portable Webcore Phonograph so that I could better enjoy listening to music that I loved. Before I got this new phonograph, I was limited to listening to only 78 rpm records on a small portable single speed record player that my cousin had given me. Prior to getting my Webcore, I listened to hits by Guy Lombardo such as Menagra Nicaragua, and Buddy Clark singing his hit song called "Linda". I suspect I loved this last hit because of my relationship with my close cousin whose name was also Linda.

My new Webcore was a multiple speed unit that could handle not only 78 rpm records, but also 45 and 33 1/3 rpm's as well. This Webcore expanded my universe of listenable music so that I could also play LP records on the relatively new format, 33 1/3 rpm, that was introduced by Columbia in 1948, at about the same time that RCA introduced the 45rpm, 7" disc.

I recall receiving an offer in the mail for a classical music LP from a company called Music Treasures of the World. It cost me a dime, including shipping, and featured two classics, one by Beethoven, his 5th symphony, and on the flip side, Schubert's 8th symphony. When the record arrived, and lifted the top of the Webcore, placed the new LP on the turntable, and hit the play button. Within a few minutes of listening to this new kind of music (classical), I was "hooked".

Although my interest in music includes all categories with the exception of Gregorian Chants, Hard Rock, and the most recent called Rap, classical music has remained my favorite. Over the years, my collection of music has grown to over 1000 records, plus tapes and CD's, covering all categories of music from serious classical composers like Mozart, Beethoven and Hayden, to the lighter composers like Rimsky Korsakov and Tchaikovsky. My collection is not only of the classics, but covers all genres of music including Broadway Musicals like "Fidler on the Roof", the "Sound of Music" and "My Fair Lady" western or "cowboy" music with performers like Glen Campbel and John Denver, a large assortment of background theme music from the movies, like the James Bond series, Born Free, and Moon River, from the hit *Breakfast At Tiffany's*, music from the "Big Band Era" featuring music by Tommy and Jimmy Dorsey and Glen Miller, as well as LP's and CD's featuring music from leading performers and composers like Perry Como, Barry Manilow, Billy Joel, Henry Mancini and Montovani.

The only problem with the LP is that it is easily damaged, particularly if something is dropped on the disc like the playing stylus or some other object. In too many cases, the damage cannot be undone and when the record is played, the stylus will skip either forward or back. When the skipping is back to an earlier groove, one must go over to the record player and manually advance the stylus beyond the damaged groove. This can be particularly annoying if it occurs repeatedly on a given LP and you are not near the player. The term "he sounds like a broken record" is used to refer to a person who repeats himself like a needle skipping backward on a damaged record. Also, as the diamond stylus "cuts" it way through the relatively soft plastic (vinyl) record removing some of the plastic, so that as the record is played repeatedly, the sound quality deteriorates with each playing. There are two tricks that serious music lovers use to avoid this problem. The first is to use the best cartridge/stylus system that you can afford. Unfortunately, a very good unit can cost hundreds of dollars. A stylus, that is replaceable, can last up to 1000 playings of LP's so that, depending on how often you play your records, it can last a year or more. The second, that very few people use, is to play the LP only once, and record the content to a CD or tape (cassette). In this way, the LP is preserved since it is only played to make the original transfer to CD or tape, and the LP can be stored for future use if the copy is lost or damaged.

My new Webcore not only enabled me to expand my interests in music, but also opened the door to new friends, many of whom I met when I joined a youth group called Club Chaverim ("Friends"). This new youth group had been formed by a vibrant new rabbi, David Hartman, who was hired by the leaders of Congregation Anshe Amas on 222 st in the Bronx to rejuvenate the synagogue.

This small portable Webcore Phonograph had another profound effect on my life since it led more or less directly to my meeting Judy Herman, a 14 year old teenager who was a member of Club Chaverim. Unbeknownst to me at the time, Judy was to become my first girlfriend and the love of my life since we went together for seven years and were married in 1962. We are still together after 68 years.

Little did my dad know back in 1955 that his gift of a Webcore Phonograph would change my life forever.

How I Almost Flunked The Ny State History Regents Exam

092120

In New York State every high school student who was in the academic program must take and pass a statewide exam, known as a Regents Exam, after completing any major course. These exams are given at the end of each semester in every major subject including math, science, english, languages such as Spanish, French, Latin, etc., and history. Each exam is three hours long and is given at each student's high school. The exams begin at 9am and end at noon. History is the most difficult because a single three hour Regents Exam covers the material in four years of history classes. If a student fails to pass any Regents Exam, and wants to get credit for having taken the subject in question, he or she must take the last semester again then take the Regents Exam after completing the course. It is particularly important to pass the Regents Exams for courses that are required to be admitted to college. In short, in the 1950's, flunking a Regents Exam in any major such as math, english or history, will delay your graduation from high school and prevent you from starting college.

In the last semester of 1958, my girl friend Judy Herman (who became my wife in June of 1962) and I, both took the final semester in history, and were preparing to take the four year history Regents Exam in June. I was reasonably good in history, even though it was far from my favorite subject, but Judy, was not very good in history and was terribly afraid of not passing the history Regents Exam.

Since no one had any idea regarding what would be on the three hour history regents that they would be taking, most students used old copies of the history Regents Exams to review and possibly help them prepare for the exam they would be taking. Since both Judy and I had been accepted to attend college in the fall, it was critical that we passed every Regents Exam that we were required to take. As a result, we spent almost a month reviewing our notes, textbooks and old Regents Exams for each major subject that we had completed in that final semester.

We spent time at Judy's apartment and at my parent's home, studying for the Regents Exams we would be taking at the end of June. We were both quite good in most subjects like math and science, but were fearful of history since it is pure memorization and not logic. I was also concerned about passing the regents in spanish since it, like history, is basically memorization. Also, I did not like spanish since I planned to study electrical engineering at CCNY and did not see any practical use for it. Unfortunately, taking at least one foreign language as a major and passing its Regents Exam, was a requirement for college admittance. Further, like history, each foreign language Regents Exam covered either two or three years of coursework in each chosen language. As a result, I spent a great deal of time studying for the Spanish Regents Exam and was not that concerned about history. Since Judy was very concerned about the history regents, I spent a great deal of time helping her study for the history Regents Exam. We spent the better part of a month both after school and on weekends studying for the Regents Exams we would be taking.

When the big day came for the Regents Exam in history, Judy and I took the bus to Evander Childs (our high school), wished each other good luck, kissed goodbye, and each went to our respective assigned classrooms for the history exam.

At 9AM sharp, a bell rang and the Regents Exams, that were delivered by armed guards that arrived in Brinks trucks, were distributed to the students. Interestingly, throughout NY state, the same exam was distributed at each high school on the same day and at the same time. In this way, there could be no cheating by enabling students to get the exams in advance and study for the actual questions that would be asked.

The three hours zipped by and before we knew it, the bell rang again signaling noon, and our little blue books, into which we had written narratives responding to the history topic we had to write about, were collected. There were two other parts to the exam that that had been collected earlier. including a multiple choice part. When the exam ended, we were allowed to take the multiple choice question sheet with us.

Students gathered outside each classroom and discussed their answers to the multiple choice part of the exam. When I met Judy she was in tears because very few of her fellow students had chosen the answers that she had. She was very much afraid that she would not pass the Regents Exam and would have to go to summer school and repeat both the last semester in history and take the Regents Exam again at the end of the summer. We took the bus home, but Judy was very quiet.

When she got home, she again shed tears when she told her mother about the exam and what had happened afterward.

The following day, we went back to Evander to get our history Regents Exam results. As we approached the bulletin board on which the grades for the Regents Exam were posted, Judy's history teacher approached her and said: "Miss Herman, come here. Couldn't you have gotten one more point?". Judy burst into tears and said: "For one more point I failed the regents and will have to go to summer school and take the Regents Exam again?". He said, "What do you mean failed the exam, you got an 89, the highest score in the school. For one more point you would have gotten a 90 which would be an A."

We then went to the next board to see my grade for the history Regents Exam. It was only a 73. A few points lower, and I would have flunked! It's funny how things sometimes work out. Judy the poor history student gets the highest grade in the school, and I, the better history student got the far lower grade and almost had to spend the summer repeating both the last semester in history and taking the Regents Exam at the end of the summer. Fortunately, we both got passing grades and went on to college that fall.

"I Hate People In General But Love Them In Particular"

August 22, 2014

I was born in New York City in 1940 and lived there till our young family moved to Bucks County, PA in August of 1966. This article is about how the multitudes of people in NYC affected me, one of the reasons we left in 1966 and never looked back, and how "my take" on people changed in the later years of my life.

Growing up in New York City, the Bronx in particular, had a profound effect on my life and the attitude I developed regarding the people in NY I encountered almost on a daily basis. When I was a pre-teenager, my parents often took me to Coney Island to spend hot sunny days on the beach and swimming in the Atlantic Ocean. I can vividly remember how crowded it became on the beach by about 11AM and how it seemed that virtually everyone in NYC was on the beach trying to escape the heat. In the 1940's and 50's air conditioning in homes and apartments was virtually unknown, so the only way to get away from the heat was to go to the beach or a free city park like Tibbets Brook or Pelham Bay. The most popular beach accessible to folks in the Bronx was Orchard Beach since getting to Coney Island, located in southern Brooklyn, was by spending an hour or so on the subway or driving for close to an hour to get there by private car, each way! Getting to orchard beach was generally just a short bus ride for most people, so this was a very popular beach, but also very crowded on a hot summer day.

Since I had to use both public busses and the subway to get virtually anywhere in the city, I was always surrounded by throngs of people. During non-rush hours, the busses and trains were OK, but early in the day and late in the afternoon, it was a struggle to use these transportation facilities. The subways in particular were a real challenge since the platforms, particularly in mid-Manhattan, would jam up with people trying to get home from work. The city actually hired people to stand on the train platforms and, while the trains were stopped and loading, would push people onto the train to pack each car up to the hilt. I can recall, as a teenager, when I had to commute to and from 14th street (Union Square) during the morning and evening rush hours, standing on the train platform and hoping that the crowds would not push me off the platform and onto the tracks!

The subways, in addition to being crowded, were hot, dirty and noisy, particularly during the rush hours. It was not too bad in the mornings, when I boarded the train at 233rd street and White Plains Road, since the trains were relatively empty and filled as the trains headed south toward Manhattan, but were jammed when I had to board the train at about 5PM at 14th street. I generally used the "IRT" branch, which stood for "Intercity Rapid Transit", but also used the

"IND" (Independent line), particularly when I attended City College of New York (CCNY) in the late 1950's and early 60's while working toward my bachelors degree in electrical engineering. To get away from the crowds and heat of the subway cars, I almost always found a space outside of the passenger compartments on the small metal "shelf" above the couplings that connected one car to the next. It was on the same level as the passenger compartment just beyond the door at the end of each car. Here, in this "private" space, there were generally no passengers, since they were not supposed to be there, it was cooler and I was not squeezed in by people. Although I had to bear the noise of the subway cars moving through the small subway tunnel, it was better than the crowded subway cars themselves. Although I did this for many years, I cannot recall even one mishap. These spaces between cars were protected by the close shelf that I stood on, and a chained guard rail to the left and right of me, so unless I was really careless, it was actually relatively safe. If I was found by a subway worker, I was generally asked to leave, but I cannot recall this happening very often.

In 1956, I worked for a small diner on 15th street and 4th avenue, called the Dineer. I delivered coffee, donuts and sandwiches to the people who worked in offices near our restaurant, and generally made a small salary and nickel and dime tips. I worked there in the summer, six days a week and on Saturdays in the winter months. After that summer, I worked for a photofinishing company called Berkey Photo, located on 13th street just west of 4th ave, where I worked first on the production floor and then, for my last two summers, providing assistance in the office. On both jobs, I was surrounded by people, both on the job and in the streets. Fortunately, I lived with my parents in the central Bronx, near the southern entrance to the Bronx Zoo, for the first twelve years of my life then for the next ten years in the northeast Bronx, known as the Edenwald section (near 233rd street and white plains road). Both areas were not as crowded as the southern Bronx or Manhatten, however, I was still always in the presence of lots of people. In short, I got to literally hate the multitudes that I had to interface with almost daily, hence, I coined the phrase: "I hated people in general".

Interestingly, my most fond memories of my childhood relate to the outings that I took with my parents and immediate family when we got into our car, and literally escaped from the city. During the spring, we picnicked in either city parks, or parks outside of the city itself. One was called Tibbets Brook Park, located just outside of the city in Yonkers and others like Tallman State Park, and Davies Lake, were in New York State, but outside of the city. When Coney Island began to change, we switched to Jones Beach State Park on the south shore of Long Island, where the beach was less crowded, and the people more to our liking. It wasn't till my teen years that I began to learn that there were other places to have fun other than in the city, and other places to live, where the people seemed somewhat "different" from those in the city. My main observation was that those who lived outside of NYC seemed nicer and friendlier than those in who lived in the city and worked there. Also, the pace of life seemed to be somewhat slower in places outside of the city where I lived.

In 1962, my highschool sweetheart and I were married and lived in an apartment on Hull Avenue just off Gun Hill Road in the Bronx. We started traveling during the warmer months and soon learned that we were not "city people" since we preferred to leave the city to get away from the crowds and enjoy the open space of the country. We vacationed in New England during my two week vacations and swam outside the city on warm summer weekends at Jones Beach on the south shore of Long Island. Although we almost purchased a home on Long Island, we decided to leave the city and live in a more suburban community and settled in Lower Bucks County in Pennsylvania, about 30 miles north of center city Philadelphia.

I guess it was in my 30's, a few years after leaving New York City, that I began to "connect" with people. Not people in general, but people in particular. My wife and I began building new relationships with people and by the time I was in my 50's, found that it was easy and enjoyable to spend time with individuals and build friendships. I am not sure this would have happened had we chosen to remain in New York, but found that it happened almost automatically when we lived in a rural setting.

I am now in my early eighties, and find that we have a wide scope of friends that we get together with on a fairly frequent basis and really enjoy being with. I believe that our friends feel as positive as we do about our relationships. I am very pleased that things turned out as they did because I truly feel that second only to ones health, the relationships one has with others are the most important things in life. I have developed the philosophy that having money is important since money can buy choices and a degree of freedom that you most likely would not have if you did not have some wealth, but my wife and I truly feel that our personal ties to others are much more important since money will not by friendship.

In summary, although I started out *hating people in general, I love people in particular*, since it is the personal relationships in our lives that really make life worth living.

It's Time To Thank Our Engineers And Scientists

11/11/15

There was a time, thousands of years ago, when mankind consisted of many small tribes that were spread over the earth, and in most cases were isolated from one another. The people of that time lived in caves or small huts made of wood, straw, sand or clay. To just survive, they had to depend on one another for food, shelter, and protection from wild animals. They were the hunters and gatherers of the early age of man.

As the world's population grew, the structure of civilization began to change so that man had more time to think and create ways to make life easier and safer. Man came to the realization that it was more efficient for some to specialize in providing food, for others protection, and for others to build and maintain the structures that provided protection from the elements. We gradually evolved into those who grew food (farmers), those who looked for animals to kill and eat (hunters), those who provided clothing for warmth (tailors), those who designed, built and maintained the dwellings that man lived in (builders and architects), and many others who provided man with what he needed to live and survive in comfort.

To keep things running in harmony, a system of payment for goods and services gradually evolved from one based on bartering (exchanging goods and services as payment) into one which was based on payment in an agreed upon system of money whose value was determined by a complex system, that eventually became almost impossible to understand. To earn the money needed to pay for things, people did work for others and were rewarded for their efforts by payment in terms of money (wages).

As things proceeded, the world became more and more complex. In the mid-eighteenth century, something called the industrial revolution took place during which the complexity of things took a giant leap forward. Machines were created to accomplish tasks that made getting things done easier and more efficient. A system of factories evolved in which people worked with machines to make many things that previously were made by hand using tedious and time consuming methods. People were paid in money (wages) for their work in these factories.

In the twentieth century, another revolution took place known as the technological revolution. The prelude to the technological revolution occurred in the late nineteenth century when batteries were developed that could store energy and produce something called electricity. This was followed with the development of electric motors, generators, and the electric light bulb. The discovery and development of the electric light bulb in itself was a revolation since up till that time, light was produced by burning oil and candles.

A new "race" of people evolved who were the ones who developed these new technological innovations and then worked on their further improvement, application, and maintenance. They were called engineers and scientists. Although they existed in small numbers prior to the technological revolution, and by the twentieth century, they became the ones who helped mankind take a giant leap forward. Their efforts resulted in the development of the vacuum tube, radio, television, the transistor, the integrated circuit, the computer, and the internet. Their efforts resulted in our traveling into space, putting satellites into orbit and visiting the moon and Mars (manned and unmanned space flights). Their breed also was responsible for the development and mass production of the automobile, and the airplane and virtually everything we use. If we become sick and have to visit a doctor or spend time in a hospital, we have a much better chance of getting well again because of the medical instrumentation and test devices that have been developed by the creative and inventive minds of our scientists and engineers. Schools began turning out large numbers of these intelligent beings so that they could enter the work force, and help create new and exciting "things" to further increase man's ability to live in safety and comfort and to provide a form of entertainment to occupy man's leisure time, something that he did not have much of in earlier times.

Unfortunately, this new breed of thinkers and innovators were to pay a heavy price for their efforts.

Two elements in the nature of man that can create problems for those with exceptional creative talents are the ego and jealousy. For too many individuals, the *ability to appreciate* what others are capable of creating, that they cannot, is lacking. Their egos and jealousy prevent them from doing this. The result in many cases is a lack of appreciation for what others have created or accomplished.

Further, those who lack these abilities often go out of their way to try to discredit or "bring down" the creative ones. This conflict can manifest itself in many ways and circumstances. At work for example, in companies with poor management, the creative ones are not given the recognition they deserve or the salary rewards that should match their contributions. Often, the management of the company and those in sales and marketing receive the greatest rewards (money), while those who are actually creating what the managers manage and what the sales people sell, receive a significantly lesser reward. When the "hard times" come, and sales fall off, it is often the creative ones who pay the heavy price of losing their jobs rather than those in management, marketing or sales. This unfair practice of "punishing" the creative ones continues to exist even today.

An additional price that the creative ones pay, is a lack of recognition in many cases for what they have created. In addition, when something does not work out as planned, it is often the creative ones who are blamed for the failures when often it is the managers who are responsible for creating the problem through faulty management decisions.

I am one of those creators or our time, an engineer, and I am one of those unsung heroes that, over the course of my forty-plus year career, did not receive the recognition and credit that I earned. I worked in many different technical areas, but cannot recall ever receiving rewards that even came close to the innovations that I created or the problems that I solved, in too many cases, single handedly.

We have a Secretaries Day, Mothers Day, Fathers Day, Labor Day, Memorial Day, Veterans Day, and even a day to recognize a rodent called Groundhogs Day, but we do not have a single day or minute to recognize those who create things and make a better world for us all. We need a day or week to recognize the creative ones who make so much possible for the rest of us. Let's think about another day to be added to those that already exist. Let's call it "Technology Day" or "Technology Week", to recognize and give thanks to those who have made our lives better through their efforts.

Landscape Painting: A Great Way To Add Beauty To The World and Create a Lasting Legacy

2/10/18

I was always pretty good at drawing and sketching, and in the 1970's I started doing simple paintings using oil based paints. turpentine was used as the thinner and needless to say, the odor was hard to take. Luckily, very little of it was used and it was tolerable.

I created a few simple paintings, but nothing to speak of. Due to my career and family life, there was little time left for me to follow this interest, so for about 30 years, my painting efforts were put on the shelf and nothing was done.

When I retired in 2006, I decided to resume my painting efforts and added it to the list of activities I decided to engage in. I remembered the smell of the early days with turpentine and decided to look into using acrylic paints instead. Luckily, this medium is widely available, is water based, it is relatively easy to work with, it is low cost, and, perhaps most importantly, there is no odor! I went to Wal-Mart, Michaels and AC Moore and bought an assortment of acrylic paints, several inexpensive assortments of brushes and some canvases to get me started. At home, I found a pallet that I had made of clear acrylic and decided to use it.

Since we have a little cabin in the Poconos, and it was a great place to work, I decided to make this my "studio". Actually, there was no studio because the cabin is very tiny, so in the warmer weather, usually between May and September, I would set up my painting stuff on a small circular table on our deck and just paint outside. When the weather was colder, I would set my stuff up on the small dining table in our all purpose room and just paint there.

Over the years since retiring, I probably did over 100 paintings. Several of them are at my daughter Joy's house in Churchville, mostly all in one room. She calls this exhibit of paintings "The Rubin Gallery". When we visit her, I enjoy looking at this array of paintings one of which is a famous scene in Central Park. It has a small stream and a bridge with the tall buildings of Manhattan in the background. When I gave here this particular painting, she exclaimed: "Dad, I walked on that bridge when I was in New York". Needless to say, I was thrilled!

My wife Judy and I moved into an over 65 community in the fall of 2019 and in addition to a formal art gallery that has a rotating exhibit of artists from off campus, there is a resident art gallery that enables the residents to display their painting and sculpture creations. I have exhibited several of my landscape paintings in this gallery and hope to continue doing so as we go forward.

To the reader of this article: If you are even minimally interested in painting, but feel it is something that may interest you, I highly recommend going to the art supply section of one of the above noted stores and purchasing some acrylic paints, some inexpensive brushes, and a pallet (or make one out of plexiglass or wood) and some thick paper. Pick a scene you like from a calendar, a photograph, or perhaps a painting you like, sketch it on paper, get some water, and start painting. Perhaps you will discover that painting is not just fun, but also relaxing. Further, because I do strictly landscape paintings, it helps people who look at my work project themselves into a scene and just "drop out".

Further, since the resulting paintings are more or less permanent, it is also a way to build a legacy that folks will enjoy when you are no longer around.

Leaving New York

A True Short Story by: Norman Rubin

I was born in the Bronx, New York, in 1940, and spent the first twenty six years living there. I married my high school sweetheart in 1962 and we had our first child, Joy Dawn, while we were living in the Bronx. I attended CCNY school of engineering and graduated in January 1963 with a degree in Electrical Engineering, six months after our marriage in June of 1962.

My first job as an engineer was in Westbury, on Long Island, about 35 minutes from where I lived with my new wife at 3339 Hull Avenue in the Bronx. We lived on the third floor of a six storey apartment building about one half block from Gun Hill Road. It was in the northeast Bronx about 2 miles from the city line between NYC and Westchester (Yonkers). The name of the company I worked for in Westbury was Digital Electronics, Inc., and was located just off the Long Island Expressway. I recall it being very close to the Westbury Music Fair and a company called Hi Temp that made Teflon covered wire. While working for Digital, I met people who lived outside the city and seemed very nice. More importantly, I had the opportunity to travel for Digital as well as other companies that I worked for later in my professional career, and had the opportunity to get to know people from all over the United States. As time went by, I realized that we have choices regarding where we want to live and work. After living in NYC and working in the areas close to the city, for about 3 years, my wife and I decided that there was a better way and started thinking about leaving the city. We actually picked out a house on Long Island, and were planning to buy it. Our problem was that every few months, the cost of the house went up and we were always just short of having enough money for the down payment. I also developed the philosophy that there were two kinds of people that had two entirely different likes and dislikes. One I referred to as "The Country Mouse" and the other as "The City Mouse". The Country Mouse lived where there were few people, but there were lots of cows, chickens, lots of grass and trees and lots of space while the City Mouse knew and liked paved streets, no grass or trees, loved being immersed in other mice, and never saw a cow or chicken. The country mouse lived in a barn while the city mouse lived in the wall of a city apartment. My wife and I loved the outdoors and loved to go picnicking, and swimming at the city parks. We found ourselves generally leaving the city to go where it was more open and green. In short, we were like the Country Mouse.

In early 1966, while I was working for my third company called EDO in College Point NY, just off the Grand Central Parkway on the Queens side of the Whitestone Bridge, I developed an interest in the Bio-medical Engineering Field. Up till that point in my career, I had worked primarily on projects funded by the Department of Defense and was then doing Sonar System work for the Navy. Although the work was both interesting and challenging, I wanted to shift into something where I could feel that people were benefiting more directly from my work. At that time, the Bio-Medical Engineering field was in its infancy and appealed to me greatly. The thought of easing pain and making peoples lives better through the application of electronics was very appealing. As a result ot my shift in interest, I began reading articles and papers on this topic and began seeking opportunities in this relatively new field. Also, my wife and I decided that we wanted to leave the city and hopefully find a better place to raise our new family. Our only child at that time was Joy, who was approaching two years old.

In the summer of 1966, I interviewed for a position with the American Optical Company and received a decent offer from them. They were located in the Chelsea section of Boston with a planned move to Chelmsford, in the NW suburbs, just off route 128. Unfortunately, they needed me to start work immediately, but because of other obligations we were unable to leave soon enough for them, so the offer was retracted and I had to resume my search for another new position.

In June of that summer, I contacted the National Institutes of Health (NIH) in Bethesda Md, and was scheduled to interview with them for a research position, however, the job placement agency I was working with at the time managed to find two companies in my field of interest that were located in the suburbs of Philadelphia. Since I would have to foot the bill for the NIH interview and we had very little money at the time, I chose to delay my interview with them and pursue to two opportunities closer to NY that the placement agency had set up. The reasons were simple: all expenses were covered and I could interview both companies in one day.

I packed a suitcase for an overnight stay and on a Sunday in July, drove down to the Trevose PA area and checked into the George Washington Motel near Street Road and US Rt. 1. I recall arriving in the late afternoon, checking into the motel, then driving down route 1 toward northeast Philadelphia. I left route 1 to explore what I thought was a typical neighborhood, but got very discouraged when I ran into dirty streets, boarded up row homes, and what appeared to be slums that seemed to go on forever!

After an hour or so of wandering around in these run-downed neighborhoods, I got something to eat at a diner on RT 1 somewhere near Red Lion Road, and returned to my motel room to bed down for the night before my two scheduled interviews on Monday.

In the morning I drove down to the Willow Grove area and interviewed with a company on Terwood Drive just off Davisville Rd. I don't recall the name of the company or anything about this interview. I grabbed a quick lunch at a diner at the corner of Old York Rd., and Terwood and proceeded to drive up to Trevose for a meeting at the Norden facility that was then located on Street Rd. The actual interview was with their medical department known as *Telemedics* that was located a few miles away on Churchville Lane, just below the Churchville Reservoir. I spent the afternoon interviewing with the Telemedics department, and was interviewed primarily by the department manager. The interview went well, and about a week later, I received an offer to join them as a design engineer. Coincidentally, I also received an offer from the company I had interviewed that morning, but decided to consider the offer from Telemedics more seriously, however, there was a major catch. I knew very little about the area and based on my travels the day before and observing the less than desirable areas in NE Philadelphia, I was not too happy about moving my family to an area that we might not like.

Right after the offer arrived from Telemedics, I decided to make another trip to the Bucks County with my wife Judy and check things out. We left our daughter with Judy's mom and took a day to drive back to Lower Bucks County and check things out in more detail. On this visit, we were pleasantly surprised with what we found. Instead of going south toward Philadelphia, we drove up into Bucks County and checked out Feasterville and the surrounding areas. We were very pleasantly surprised and even found an apartment complex known as Trevose Square Apartments on the corner of Brownsville and Street Roads that seemed perfect for us. We were so impressed with what we found in general, that I decided to accept the job offer, put down a deposit on the apartment, and move away from New York.

We moved toward the end of August, and I started working immediately for Telemedics. Our apartment was not ready till after Labor day, so we spent a week at the George Washington Motel then moved into our 1 year old apartment in Trevose Square Apartments.

As soon as we moved there, I immediately noticed a difference in the people. Although we were only about 30 miles from downtown Philadelphia, the people seemed more courteous and patient. The pace seemed to be a bit slower than in New York.

We moved into our new apartment at Trevose Square just after Labor Day and immediately began to make new friends of our neighbors on our floor and the floor above us. The apartment complex included a pool and each apartment had a balcony that overlooked grass and trees. We spent a year living at Trevose Square and it was like one big party. We were always getting together with our neighbors for simple get togethers or we would have parties involving several of our neighbors. In short we fell in love with our new area, and within six months decided that this was the place for us. We found a sample (model) home we liked, purchased a one half acre lot in a new development in Churchville, and moved into our new home at the end of September 1967. We lived in that home for 52 years. Our kids grew up in it, and when we think of New York, it is hard to believe that we ever lived there.

Lost Faith In One Night

Aug 8, 2014

This story is not about me, but my grandfather on my father's side of the family.

Sam Rubin, my grandfather, was born and raised in the Ukraine in the latter part of the 19th century. He had a medium sized family with brothers and sisters, and was raised following the orthodox Jewish tradition. He was very close to his religious, and in fact, as he related it to me, was studying the Talmud as a teenager, in preparation for him becoming a rabbi. His entire family slept in one bedroom and had a small liquid fuel heater to heat their small home. It was most likely a small portable kerosene heater.

On one particular night, the entire family went to sleep and since it was cold outside, they lit the kerosene heater and went to sleep. When my grandfather awoke the next morning, he looked around him and noticed that everyone in the room seemed to still be sleeping. Oddly, he detected the strong smell of kerosene. When he checked the heater, he observed that it was no longer lit. He immediately thought this was odd and proceeded to check out his family that he thought up till this point was just asleep. On closer examination and shock, he noticed that none of them were breathing. He tried shaking each one with the hope that they would waken, but with no success. He quickly ran out into the street to get help, but it was to no avail. All of his family members were no longer alive.

It turned out that some time during the early morning hours, after the family had gone to sleep, the kerosene heater had failed, but continued to expel deadly fumes that killed his entire family, *except for him.*

My grandfather lost his religion that night. He could not understand or accept what had happened and how a god, if one existed, could allow such a thing to happen to a family that followed all of the orthodox laws and practices. He also could not understand why he alone was spared to have to endure the agony of what had happened.

My grandfather lived to be ninety six. Throughout his life, he never stopped asking *"why"*. He most likely died still asking why. Further, he never followed Judiasm or any religion from that fateful night on. Because of what had happened when that heater failed and took his family from him, he lost his faith in his religion or any religion for that matter, and always continued to question the existence of any god.

He met my grandmother in the Ukraine, they married, and then, because of the religious persecution that was rampant toward the end of the 1800's in Russia and the Ukraine, (the pogroms), he decided to leave his homeland and build an new life in the United States.

He left the Ukraine in 1905 and, while my grandmother was carrying their first child, my father Milton Rubin, traveled alone in the hold of a ship (steerage), to start a new life in America. He immigrated to the USA and passed through Ellis Island along with tens of thousands of other European immigrants who also left Europe because of religious and political problems that were prevalent there at that time. He chose Brooklyn, NY as the place to start, and started earning a living as a cabinet maker's apprentice. Within a year or so, he earned enough money for my grandmother and father, who was now about a year old, to join him in Brooklyn. They made the trip in 1906, also as steerage passengers, and started a new life in America.

I had a great deal of respect for my grandfather and spent many hours as a child and teenager engaged in long discussions on life and philosophy with him. He was a true pioneer who lost his entire family in the Ukraine because of a faulty heater, left eastern Europe, and started a new life in Brooklyn. When my grandparents saved a little money, they bought a grocery store in Brooklyn and ran it for several years. When things did not work out as planned in Brooklyn, he got on a bus with my dad and traveled about 100 miles northwest of New York City to a small town called Liberty. They found and bought a 115 acre farm in Liberty NY, and started all over again, trying to hack out a living as a vegetable farmer with a few cows and chickens. When this failed to provide an adequate living, he and my grandmother, who was a great cook, started taking in borders and probably started the B&B business (Bed and Breakfast). They literally built a 3 storey hotel building to accommodate their growing hotel business and ran it successfully for over 20 years. I can recall, with very fond memories, my summers as a child at the hotel, and its fresh water "swimming area".

My grandparents sold their hotel business in 1947 after offering it to their children, who had no interest in owning and running a hotel. During their 20 years or so in the hotel business, they brought a great deal of pleasure to thousands of families, mostly from NY City, who came to the "Borscht Belt" in the Catskills, to get away from the heat and diseases that were prevalent in the cities at that time. Tuberculosis (TB) was a major problem from the mid 1800's until the middle of the 20th century in the heavily populated cities until a cure and preventative vaccine was developed that gradually erased this dreaded disease.

After selling the hotel business, my grandparents moved closer to the town of Liberty and retired to a small three storey home where they lived until 1956, when they moved back to Booklyn and lived with my aunt Fannie until they died.

As noted before, my grandfather, Sam Rubin, was a highly intelligent man who, in spite of loosing his family, leaving his native homeland in the Ukraine, starting a new life in New York, and living the life of a modern age pioneer, lived a full and rich life until he died at the age of 96 of a very rare disease. His death certificate read: Cause of Death: *Old Age*. I feel privileged to have known him and to have been his grandson.

Me, A Salesman?

Jan 26, 2015 (rev1)

After working in the disability field, and applying my skills as an engineer by helping people of all ages with special needs for 11 years, I developed a great deal of knowledge and information about devices and equipment that could help people in this special category. I had also developed very close relationships with the "movers and shakers" in this small field. In particular, I got to know the owners of several small companies who had developed unique items for the special needs field. One of these companies sold only a single product known as "The Discrete Trial Trainer", a very powerful and unique computer program for individuals with Autism. I also developed an interest in the products made by four other companies that I dealt with that were designed to help those with communication issues and special education needs. One of the companies was called the *Tool Factory* that carried products made by several companies who specialized in special needs software.

At this time, I was getting somewhat restless and wanted to expand my horizons, so it occurred to me that I might be of value to these five companies by possibly representing them in my geographical area. Or expressed in another way, becoming their local representative who, after being furnished with "leads", or prospective customers for their products, would visit these customers to demonstrate the particular product or products of interest, provide product literature and answer questions. Over a year or so, and numerous discussions with each of the leaders of these companies, it was agreed that I would become their local representative.

I started working part-time on this new endeavor by visiting companies late in the day, or on Saturday's if possible. After a year of so of working part time, I concluded that this was not really working very well since new sales were very slow in coming, and I was putting in lots of time on the phone, on the internet, and in my car, traveling to the various potential customers. In the winter of 2006, after much consideration, I decided that things were not working because I my efforts were only part time, and I was not giving this new challenge my "best shot".

I continued at this on a part time basis, but when I retired in May of 2006, worked at it full time. After a year, things still were not going very well even though I was working at it mostly full time. I decided that the fault was mine, so I decided to move on to other things of interest but not sales.

This turned out to be a mistake since I later learned that one must work at being a sales person for at least four years on a full time basis before things begin to be profitable. In summary, if someone reading this decides to become an independent sales person, be prepared to work at it full time for at least four years before giving up.

The Strange Connection Between Model Railroading and Apple Sauce

Jan 20, 2014

When I was eight years old, my father surprised me for the holidays that year by giving me a set of Lionel trains. When I was younger, he had given me a much simpler set that was a spring wound wind-up set that ran in a small circle pulling a few simple passenger cars. This new Lionel set was a whole different ball game since it was electric powered and enabled me to not only control the train, but also many different action accessories, including a dump car, a milk car, and electrically operated switch tracks that enabled me to route the train onto sidings. This trains set gave me my first opportunity to make things happen by "remote control". This concept fascinated me and within a few hours of playing with my new train set, I was "hooked" on this new world of what was known as "Model Railroading". The set included a Berkshire 2-8-4 steam locomotive with tender or coal car that had a remotely controlled whistle. The engine produced puffs of white smoke when small yellow smoke pills were placed into its smoke stack.

Unfortunately, when I received this Lionel train set, we lived in a two room apartment in the central Bronx, a few blocks from the now world famous Bronx Zoo, so I was limited to running the set on a slippery linoleum covered living room floor, and having to put it away each time after I was finished playing with it. Also, because the floor was very slippery, the tracks would move and often separate causing the heavy engine and cars to spill onto the floor. It was very frustrating to say the least.

When I was twelve years old, we moved into a small home in the north-east Bronx that had a garage and small, unfinished basement room. After we got settled in our new home, my dad built me a 4' by 8' train platform out of plywood and set it up in the garage. I quickly designed a two loop layout with two sidings using the two additional remote control switch tracks that my dad had purchased for me. My new layout grew to include an entire town that had streets and grass, with miniature buildings, many illuminated. After a while, I added scenery and sound effects that produced train sounds from records. I also started collecting all sorts magazines and books on railroading, and quickly became an expert on all facets of both model (small scale) and real (full scale) railroading and railroad history. By the time I was twelve, model railroading and trains became my primary hobby and I became known as a "model railroading nut". I was so obsessed with trains that I would often sit in class and sketch pictures in my workbooks of various kinds of train engines. Everyone who knew me back then, including many of my teachers, knew of my obsession with trains.

In the fall of 1952, after completing grade school, I started my three year stint at Olinville Junior High School, also known as P.S. 113. I enjoyed most of the subjects I took there, with the exception of history and english. While taking english in the eighth grade at Olinville, something very funny happened relating to my interest in Model Railroading.

My english teacher, decided to have some fun with the class, and give us a chance to engage in a little exercise involving impromptu public speaking. At the start of each class, the teacher would randomly select a student to go the front of the class. The teacher would then select a subject that the student would have to speak on for about three minutes, without any preparation. When the three minutes were up, the teacher would signal the student to stop and return to his/her seat. The teacher would then grade the student on how the subject was handled. This went on for several days, until finally, my name was called.

I slowly rose from my seat and went up to the front of the the class and waited while the teacher thought of a subject for me to speak about. The teacher, who knew of my great interest in trains and model railroading, thought for a few seconds, turned to me and said: "I have to think of something that is as far from trains and model railroading as I can". After about thirty long seconds of what appeared to me to be deep contemplation, with a big grin on her face, she looked me right in the eye and slowly said: "Apple Sauce". I believe she chose this topic because she wanted to "stump" me.

I looked at her for a few seconds, and then began to speak-

"Apple sauce is a tasty treat that can be served as a dessert or used as a side dish. It is made from apples of various varieties that give apple sauce distinctive flavors, and sugar is generally, but not always, added to sweeten the apple sauce. Apples grow on apple trees, and they have to be picked after they ripen so that they can be made into pies, baked, eaten raw, or made into apple sauce.

At this point, I hesitated and glanced over at my teacher and notice that she had a puzzled look on her face. The class however was firmly focused on me and was eagerly waiting for me to continue with my presentation, so I continued.

A few years ago, my family and I drove to Liberty, New York, in the early fall to visit my grandparents. It was a cool but beautiful sunny late September day when we arrived at my grandparent's home. We had lunch and then the grownups decided that it would be a perfect afternoon for the entire family to visit the old apple orchard that my grandparents owned, and pick some apples so that my grandmother could make applesauce and prepare some fresh apple pies, so we piled into two cars and drove out into the country toward the orchard.

The orchard was over 50 years old, and had many stately Cortlandt and MacIntosh apple trees that were growing on the side of a hill in the orchard. I could clearly see the small babbling brook that ran through the orchard at the bottom of the hill with clear cold fresh running water that meandered over small rocks in the brook as the water made its way to what was an old abandoned "swimming hole"."

All of a sudden, my teacher looked at me with an annoyed look on her face and said: "OK, that's enough, your three minutes are up. You can return to your seat." I looked at her and started to move when suddenly the entire class shouted: "Please let him finish, we want to hear the rest of his story". The teacher, with a frown on her face, slowly nodded at me, so I continued.

After parking our cars along the side of the rode next to the orchard, we all crossed over the stream on a small wooden footbridge and proceeded to head uphill toward the orchard with my little, six year old brother Mikey running ahead of us. There was a slight but pleasant breeze blowing as we proceeded up the hill into the orchard and we could see small birds darting in and out of the trees. As we got closer to the orchard, I could see the trees laden with apples, many of which had already fallen to the ground. The scene was like what you would see on a picture postcard or beautiful calendar.

Mikey was well ahead of us now and had disappeared into the orchard. I ran ahead to try to keep up with him. I glanced over my shoulder and saw my parents and grandparents slowly making their way up the hill about two hundred feet behind me. I had never picked apples before and assumed that we could just pick them off the ground, since there were hundreds just lying around, but my little brother Mikey had other ideas. I stopped running for an instant just in time to see him run over to a very old tree, grab hold of the trunk and start to climb up the tree. I guess he decided not to bother with the apples on the ground and probably thought it would be more fun to scramble up the trunk and pick apples right from the tree.

I was still about a hundred feet away but I could see him up in the tree about ten feet off the ground. He left the main trunk and started to climb out onto one of the old limbs to get to the apples, but before I could give what he was doing much thought, I heard a loud "crack", and saw my little brother Mikey and the old tree limb on which he was clinging, falling to the ground. They both hit the ground and the tree limb broke in several places. I could see apples flying everywhere. I ran over to Mikey as fast as I could, but when I got to him, he was crying loudly and holding his arm. My parents and grandparents saw what had happened and came running over as fast as they could. My dad examined Mikey's arm and realized that it was not just the tree limb that had been broken when it hit the ground. He picked Mikey gently up in his arms and we proceeded back to the parked cars as carefully and as quickly as we could.

We got into the cars, left the orchard, and headed directly back to town and right to Liberty General Hospital where Mikey was examined and his arm X-rayed. Luckily the only damage was to his arm that was broken in two places. The bones were set and his arm placed in a plaster cast. One funny thing that I will never forget was the name of the doctor who treated him. His name was "Dr. Pain". Can you imagine a doctor going through life with this name? I don't remember too much else that happened that day, but I do recall Mickey saying to me as we left the hospital; "There has to be an easier way to make applesauce."

When I finished, the teacher looked at me in a puzzled way, but she was smiling. The class applauded as I returned to my seat, something that I don't recall happening with any of the other students. I don't recall the grade that I received for my little talk on apple sauce, but felt that I did fulfill the impromptu speaking requirement even though the teacher seemed to be disappointed that she did not catch me speechless by picking a topic that she felt was in no way related to trains or model railroading.

"Mr. Fix It"

I guess it all started when I was only seven when my father bought a small automatic laundry in the Bronx at 165th st and Morris Avenue, not too far from the Yankee Stadium. It was a small nickel and dime operation with 20 Bendix front load washing machines two extractors and two driers. He bought this store after working in the Brooklyn Navy Yard as a machinist for the Navy during WW II where he designed and built things primarily out of sheet metal to be used on ships. Since we had very little money, and my father was handy at fixing things, he would do his own repairs at his laundry whenever one of the machines would fail to function properly. I helped out in the laundry on Saturdays and during the week over the summers. On Sundays, when the store was closed, I would accompany my dad when he would make repairs to the various machines. By watching him do these repairs, I learned about the various parts that made the things "tick" such as motors, transmissions, and valves and also how to work with various kinds of tools that he used in making the repairs. By the time I was in my early teens, I knew how to diagnose problems, take machines apart, replace or fix broken parts, and put the machines back together.

Fixing "stuff" may have also been in my genes since my grandfather was a "pioneer" who immigrated to America over 100 years ago and both earned a living by farming and also running a small hotel called Hotel Rubin just outside of Liberty, NY, in the Catskill mountains. He and my dad did all of the repairs on the farm and hotel to keep things running. These chores included plumbing, carpentry and electrical work as well repairing the various gasoline engines that were used on the farm and at the hotel.

I started designing and building things out of wood when I was a teenager and also loved creating and building things using my number 10½ AC Gilbert Erector Set, that I still have.

In 1962, when my wife and I got married, I bought my first car, a used 1956 Chevy Bel Air two door sedan with a 6 cylinder engine. After being "taken" a few times by my "friendly" local garage in the Bronx, I decided to take an adult education course being offered at Evander Childs HS and invest in a full set of Craftsman tools from Sears, which I still use. I soon started doing my own maintenance and auto repairs including tune ups, oil and filter changes, and tackling such things as replacing worn brake linings and exhaust system parts. I even rebuilt a few carburetors over the years. Although today's modern cars do not require the frequent maintenance of the cars of the 60's and 70's, I still change the oil and filters and do an occasional brake job.

In 1966 we left the Bronx, moved to Bucks County, and soon moved into our own new home in Churchville. My repair challenges now expanded to include our GE Washer and Drier, our fridge and electric range, a dishwasher and our oil fired heating system. We had our own well, so I quickly learned about water pumps and storage tanks to keep them operating as well. I also had both a riding lawn mower and a push type to keep going as well (oil changes, blade sharpening and tune ups).

As the family grew, I tackled several major jobs including finishing an "attic room" and converting it to a 4th bedroom by doing framing, insulation, paneling, wall board installation, electrical wiring and the installation of hot water baseboard heating. I became a master at "sweating" a copper joint and doing all types of plumbing work.

About 12 years after we moved into our home, I designed a large two car garage and hired a contractor to build it. After it was completed, I added all the lighting, electric outlets, and installed two electric garage door openers that our children bought us as a present. The existing one car garage I converted to a paneled study with custom designed and built book cases and shelves, a food pantry and a closet. Since I did not see the need to heat this study throughout the winter, I installed electric baseboard heat with its own thermostat.

We were in our home for 52 years, and used the GE washer and drier that we bought in 1967 for 45 years. They were 45 years old when they finally had to be replaced since parts were no longer available to fix them.

Over the years I have been called "Mr Fix It", "Mr. Wizard" and other various names by those who are somewhat familiar with some of the things I have worked on. Now if I can only figure out how to fix our broken government and some of the ills that keep plaguing the world, that would really be something!.

My Dad's "New Used" Washing Machine

As a result of a job change and a desire to move away from New York City and live in a more rural setting, my wife Judy, two year old daughter Joy and I relocated from the Bronx to Bucks County near where my new job was located. We chose this area because at the time we had family and many friends who still lived in or near NY City, and we did not want to break our ties with them by moving a great distance away. Since we were only about a 2 hour drive from the Bronx, we made frequent trips back to the Bronx to visit both family and friends who still lived there.

On one weekend in 1968, we made the two hour trip from Churchville to spend the day with my parents who lived in the northeast Bronx, a few blocks from the Bronx/Mount Vernon border. My mom was upstairs when we arrived and my dad was in the basement installing a "new" washing machine. Actually, it wasn't new, but was a used machine that he had purchased from a self service laundromat that had closed. It was a frontload, tumbler-type "Bendix" washer that handled a single wash load of about 8 pounds.

My dad had been in the laundromat business and had owned two stores. The first, located at 165th St. & Morris Ave, in the Bronx, that he owned from 1947 until 1955. The second store was in Mount Vernon that he owned from about 1960 until 1966. Both stores were full service as opposed to the self-service (do it yourself) stores that became popular in the late 1950's. He was forced to close his second store when a coin-operated (self service) store opened just a few doors from his. Both of the stores he had owned had the frontload Bendix washers that he had learned to service himself, since hiring a repairman each time a machine needed repairs, was a costly affair, that he could ill afford. When I had lived with my parents as a child and teenager, I worked in these two stores to "help out" during normal business hours, and also helped with the various repairs and maintenance like changing the washing machine's transmission oil and cleaning the lint traps. It was dirty, messy work, that I can't say I enjoyed.

When we arrived at my parent's home I exchanged hugs and kisses with my mom then went downstairs to the basement to say hello to my dad and see how the installation of his "new" used washing machine was coming along. From the look of his unshaven face, soiled clothes, and cigarette butts in the sink, I could tell that he had been working on installing the machine for quite a while, and from the dour expression on his face, I could clearly see that the job was not going well and that he was not in a very good mood.

I held out my hand and said: "Hi dad, how are things going?" His response was something like; "I have been working on this @#&! machine for over two days, and can't get this darn thing to start." He said that their old Bendix had finally reached a point where it no longer made sense to be repaired, and that he gotten a real good deal on this "new used" machine.

I looked at the machine and asked; "Where did you get it?" He replied; "From the owner of a self-service laundromat that he had closed and was selling everything in the store. When I got there the store was pretty much cleaned out, and I was lucky to get one of the last machines he had left. It seemed to be in great shape and the owner assured me that it was in tip-top running condition, but no matter what I do, I can't get it to start. I have checked and double checked everything but it just won't run."

I looked everything over and couldn't find anything obviously wrong with the installation. While I was scratching my head, I noticed a small box toward the top and right side of the machine with a small slot in the front and a chrome push plunger on top. The electrical line cord that was firmly plugged into the AC outlet on the wall, connected the machine to the ac outlet and went directly into this small, innocent looking little box.

After a few seconds of thought, I asked my dad; "Where did you say you bought this machine?" He repeated; "From a self-service laundromat." I looked at the small box with the slot and plunger and, after a few seconds of thought, asked if he had a quarter. He said; "Why do you want a quarter?" I repeated simply; "Please, just give me a quarter."

He reached into his pocket, and after a few seconds, came up with a handful of change. Among the change was a single quarter that he handed over to me with a puzzled look on his face. I closed the door of the machine, slipped the quarter into the slot on the front of the little white box, reached up to the top of the box, and with a little effort, pushed the small, chrome-plated plunger down. With a little jerk, the machine burst into life. The tumbler started to turn, and I could hear it filling with water. My dad just looked at me, then at the machine again with a look of both amazement and disgust.

I stood there next to my dad for a few minutes as we both watched his "new" used washing machine humming along perfectly doing exactly what it was supposed to do. I didn'twant to say anything to get him any more frustrated, but just put my hand on his shoulder to comfort him and quietly just said; "You did say you bought it from a self-service laundromat that had closed, didn't you?" I refrained from saying to him; "Aren't self-service Laundromats also called "Coin Operated Laundries?". He was very quiet for the rest of our visit, but I think he was happy that we finally got the machine to run. All it took was a quarter and a simple push of a plunger.

On the way back to Pennsylvania after our visit, a thought popped into my head about my dad's "new used" washing machine. I quietly said to my wife; "I hope he got the key to open the little coin box on his "new used" washing machine, otherwise, it may not turn out to be much of a bargain." I don't ever recall asking him if he did get a key and I don't remember him ever mentioning the washing machine again.

My Fear Of Public Speaking
– Where Did It Go?

Actually, I never had a fear of speaking in public, either with very small groups of people, or in larger groups. For as long as I can remember, I enjoyed engaging folks in conversation on a wide range of subjects, and seldom was at a loss for words. My mom used to tell everyone, that I was born talking. I doubt that this was true, but there is strong evidence that I began talking at a very early age, and also developed a fairly broad vocabulary for one so young.

When my grandparents went from farming to running a small hotel just outside of Liberty NY, my mom used to tell people that there were visitors who came back to the hotel, that was called Hotel Rubin, year after year just to be able to talk to me. Since the hotel was sold in 1947, when I had just turned 7, I must have been able to carry on intelligent discussions with grownups when I was even younger.

I can recall when I was only 8 years old and in the 3rd grade at P.S. 6 in the Bronx, when my teacher had to leave the room, she always chose me to stand in front of the class and tell them stories to keep them engaged until she returned. This was very easy for me since my dad used to read me stories from a book entitled "Grimms Fairy Tales" that my aunt Estelle had given to me as a birthday present when I was very young. When I was asked to entertain the class during my teacher's absences, I recited these tales to the class. Many years later, when I was an adult, I learned that this was not a good choice of material for bedtime stories, since these fairly tales were often very scary. In fact, I don't recall ever being afraid of these stories, and don't recall ever having difficulty sleeping because of them. I suspect I was very mature for my age, and didn't have any difficulties with them.

When in Junior High School, and had just progressed to the next grade, I recall my English teacher asking each student to get up in front of the class and tell a short story relating to a topic that she would pick on the spur of the moment. The objective was to get us to learn to speak spontaneously. At the time, I had a reputation for being a "train nut" since my primary hobby was Lionel trains, and both my classmates and teachers all knew this.

When it was my turn to speak in front of the class, the teacher, in an attempt to stump me, said: "I have to pick a topic as far from trains as I can think of." After a few minutes of careful contemplation, she blurted out with: "Apple sauce". Little did she know that I had a very long and detailed story about apples, apple picking and apple sauce. It was based on a true event that had occurred while my family and I went to Liberty to pick apples in my grandparent's 15 acre apple orchard. On that day, my brother Mikey, fell out of an apple tree in the orchard and broke his arm.

Since this story related to apple sauce, I chose to tell it to the class but about half way into the story, when my 3 minutes were up, my teacher said: "enough, you can sit down." The class immediately objected and insisted that I finish the story. Needless to say, my teacher was not a happy camper, but allowed me to finish the story.

I recall another true incident that occurred while attending engineering school at CCNY in New York. When I was in my junior year, I took a course in public debating and, for our final exam, the teacher broke the class up into pairs and each pair had to debate in front of the class on a topic that the each pair had selected. My teams topic was something called "Pay TV" that turned out to be the predecessor of what was to become Cable TV. My job was to debate the pro side of pay TV and my opponent, a graduating Senior, had to debate the negative side. My opponent's mistake was to say to me, while we met in the library while I was doing research for my side of the debate: "Boy, am I going to mop up the floor with you." On hearing this, I decided to put my full effort into winning the debate. As things turned out, I did such an effective job in delivering my side of the debate, that when the class voted on a winner, I got all of the classes votes and my opponent got zilch.

My ability to deliver information to groups publicly served my well during my professional career as an electrical engineer since on numerous occasions during my 43 years in my field, I often had to deliver information in front of groups of all sizes and in all sorts of places.

One famous true story occurred when I had to travel to France to attend a conference held in an outskirt of Strassburg. At this conference, a competitor presented a paper on a system that could have resulted in an international specification being altered to favor his system and hurt the sales of one that I had designed and that was the mainstay of my companies product line. The organizer of the conference,. whose name was Steve, offered me the opportunity to respond, on the podium, to what the presenter was to deliver to a group of about 300 conference attendees. Since I was totally unprepared to speak at this conference, I told Steve to watch me for a thumbs-up or down while the speaker was making his delivery to the audience. I was so upset at what I heard the speaker say during his presentation, since many falsehoods were presented, I gave Steve a thumbs up. Steve proceeded to introduce me and tell the group that I was going to give an unannounced presentation on the same topic.

I went up to the podium with the few hastily written notes I had scribbled down during my opponents talk, and with my knees shaking, delivered my talk. When I was finished, much to my shock and surprise, the entire audience rose to their feet and applauded. This did not occur when my opponent had finished his paper. Later in the conference, numerous people who had heard both speeches came over to me and congratulated me on my presentation. They said that they were thankful that someone was able to respond to the falsehoods that the first speaker had relayed to the audience. It is my belief that my opponent was very sorry for ever presenting his paper since my rebuttal saved my company and literally "killed" his.

As a professional engineer, I often had to visit potential customers to which a technical proposal had been submitted, to present it and answer questions. I handled these presentations very well. On one occasion, I had written a proposal for the precision power supplies to be used in the development of the 757 and 767 aircraft. Boeing liked my proposal, but wanted a face to face interview. As a result, I flew to Seattle and presented my proposal in person and answered their questions. They were obviously impressed since they awarded my company the contract and I beat three competing west coast companies to which I later learned, Boeing was going to award the contract to. As a result, my work resulted in helping Boeing develop two aircraft that were to become the replacements for the 727. As far as I know these aircraft are still in the air.

I have a gift that enables me to present highly technical material to folks that are not necessarily technically astute. In this way, they can learn about things that would be normally be "beyond" them and gain from the newly acquired knowledge.

My last full time position was in the special needs field in which I was hired to start a new department called Assistive Technology. It was located in Langnorne, PA and was known as Woods Services (formerly known as The Woods School). Over the 11 year period that I was there, I gave presentations to both employees of Woods as well as at conferences throughout the world. Here again, my public speaking abilities served me well.

When I retired in 2006, I continued for a short time, in the sales field where again, I had to make presentation, primarily on a one on one basis. Again, my ability to speak clearly, and communicate with people directly, worked to my advantage. Unfortunately, this did not last because of other issues that arose in my life, so I exited this field and worked in it for only two short years.

In 2010, I stumbled on a group called REAP (Retired Engineers & Professionals) where I continued to give presentations to the group. I was always received well and people both enjoyed and learned from my presentations. Unlike work earlier in my career and life that relied primarily on the overhead projector and or flip charts, I now used Power Point as my means of presenting material, both written text and in photograph form. I love using Power Point because it has so many useful built in features that make presentations very lucid and enjoyable. I find it easy to work with as well. My hat off to Microsoft! Hey, I am typing this in their most widely used program, *Word*.

At REAP, I have made twelve presentations ranging from Space Travel, to Marilyn Monroe. Members of REAP, after hearing me present, recommended me to other groups to which I have also made presentations. I have become somewhat of a celebrity at a local library known as the Northampton Free Library in Richboro, as well as The Clymer Library in Pocono Pines.

So you see, that when I learned at CCNY in 1960, that we engineering students could pick some non-engineering electives, my selecting public speaking as an elective, turned out to be a great decision. When computers came along with the work of Microsoft, being able to present material directly perhaps using Power Point, is a real asset. I never regretted this early decision since it has served me in "spades", not only as a professional engineer, but in my private life as well. I urge you who are reading this, to grasp the opportunity to deliver presentations to groups and use power Point as the presentation medium. It will most likely serve you well in your work, and continue to serve you well when you retire, if you enjoy making presentations as I do.

In summary, I never really had a fear of public speaking, but made presentations to both large and small groups and continue to do so in my retirement.

"My Fear Of Rattle Snakes"

I was born and raised in New York City, and lived only a few blocks from the southern entrance to the Bronx Zoo. For as long as I can remember, I always had an interest in nature even though my childhood environment in the city consisted mostly of paved roads, apartment buildings, concrete sidewalks, cars, trucks, buses, subway trains and hoards of people. Except for an occasional picnic in Pelham Bay Park with my family, I had little opportunity to encounter mother nature's creatures with the exception of pigeons, cats, dogs, and unfortunately, an occasional mouse, or cockroach in our small apartment.

In the late 1940's, while watching a nature program on "Children's Theater" on our 12 inch black and white Admiral TV, I learned that there were things called rattle snakes that could bite and inject a strong venom that could kill. The snake gets its name from the rattle on its tail that it would shake before striking a victim. I recall developing an instant fear of rattle snakes but never encountered one during my 26 years in the city, except seeing them behind glass at the zoo.

In the summer of 1966, a job change brought my wife Judy and two year old daughter Joy to Bucks County where there was grass, trees, meadows and even forests, a very different environment from the Bronx. After moving to our new home in Churchville, I recall getting a copy of the *Bulletin Almanac* and reading about the flora and fauna in Pennsylvania. I gasped when I read that there were rattle snakes roaming around freely in the woods and meadows of Pennsylvania, and possibly right in Churchville. I was particularly concerned since I had become an avid gardener, and spent lots of time on our little ½ acre property, tending the trees, shrubs, vegetable and flower gardens that we had planted around our home. I was afraid of encountering a rattle snake and possibly being bitten.

We spent 52 years living in our home in Churchville, and 32 years since we bought a small cabin in the Pocono Mountains, and I have never encountered a rattle snake either at home or at our cabin in the woods in the Poconos. In the late summer of 1980, while cutting the lawn at our home in Churchville, something happened that changed my take on rattle snakes forever.

It was a typical hot, muggy August afternoon, and I was dressed in shorts, no shirt and low cut sneakers with no socks, while I cut the grass in our backyard with a push power lawn mower. At that time, we still had three apple trees on our property, and, since I never sprayed our apples since I am against using chemical pesticides), many apples had fallen to the ground and were lying there decaying all around me in the grass. Suddenly, as I walked past the fallen apples, I felt something sharp in my sneaker, like cut glass or a needle. I stopped, removed my sneaker, inverted it and saw a small insect with a black and yellow body fall out and onto the grass. It was a yellow jacket, that must have been feeding on one of the decaying apples. I must have hit the apple with my foot, and the yellow jacket fell into my sneaker and stung my foot. I had been stung by insects before, and never thought much of it, so I put my sneaker back on and continued pushing my mower to finish cutting the rear lawn

I walked about 20 feet from where I had the encounter with the yellow jacket, and suddenly began to feel very strange. I broke out into a sweat, my whole body began to itch, and I could feel my heart rate zooming up. I knew I was having a reaction to the yellow jacket sting, so I instinctively ran into the house as fast as I could and fortunately remembered the small bottle of Benedryl that we kept on the fireplace mantle in the playroom. It was there to treat a sun rash that one of our children had developed that the Benedryl seemed to keep in check. I yelled to my wife that I had been stung and to call the doctor while I grabbed the Benedryl, noting that there was only about an ounce or two left in the bottle, unscrewed the cap, and chug-a-lugged the contents of the bottle.

By now, I began to feel very faint and was having trouble breathing. I vaguely remember my wife speaking to our doctor on the phone and asking what to do. He told her to get me into the car and rush me to the hospital ASAP, and not to bother calling the emergency squad because there was no time to lose. The last thing I remember was the feeling of the cold playroom floor on my back after I had grabbed the wall and lowered myself to the floor as I slipped into unconsciousness.

Somehow, my wife and kids got me into the back of into our 1977 Chevy station wagon, and raced to St. Mary's Hospital in Langhorne, about 15 minutes from our home. The next thing I remember was a nurses hand reaching toward me in the rear of the station wagon and holding a small vile of very strong stuff (probably ammonia) under my nose. I quickly regained consciousness, was maneuvered out of the rear of the wagon, into a wheel chair and rushed into the emergency room. Since I had already taken the Benedryl, and seemed to be coming around, the doctor put me on a glucose IV drip and said that they would keep me under observation for about an hour to ensure that I did not slip back into unconsciousness. I was awake during this time but feeling very weak.

After about an hour, I was released from the hospital, but was so weak when I got home that I just got into bed and slept for the next day or so. In the days that followed, I did extensive research on insect stings and learned that when I was stung, I went into something called "anaphylactic shock", and that I had come very close to meeting our maker. Most likely, my quick assessment of what was happening right after I was stung, and having the good sense to quickly swallow the Benedryl had probably saved my life.

When they say; "Don't sweat the small stuff", don't believe it. Up until 1980, I was deathly afraid of being bitten by a rattle snake that is very rarely (if ever) seen, fairly large, is afraid of people, and, from what I have learned, does not want to bite and generally tries to avoid humans and other large animals. Further, the rattle snake has the decency to warn its victim before it strikes. On the other hand, we are surrounded by millions of crawling and/or flying insects like bees and wasps that are often less than an inch long, that will strike without warning, and their stings can be fatal. I am no longer fearful of rattle snakes, but am always careful when I go into my gardens at home, or into the fields and forests both in Churchville and in the Poconos and are always on the lookout for the "little ones" that can get you.

My High School Physics Teacher Tony Pridmore

It is interesting to note that as we progress from kindergarten through high school and for some of us college, we have literally hundreds of teachers that help us grow as individuals, but after completing each course or subject, we forget about them and generally they forget about us. This is not surprising considering the fact that, in the nineteen fifties, most teachers had about 6 classes each day, and each class had, as an average, about 30 students. This amounts to about 180 new students every 9 months during each school year. As a result, it is most likely that we may remember some of our teachers, but as the years go by, our teachers are not likely to remember us. In a few instances this general rule may not apply.

When I attended Evander Childs H.S. on Gun Hill Road in the Bronx, New York, in my Junior Year, I did something that was not recommended. I took Physics before Chemistry and met a teacher who was to become a personal and close friend. Her name was

Antoinette Pridmore who preferred to be called "Tony" Pridmore. She taught Physics at Evander and I met her when I decided to take Physics in the fall of 1956, just after I turned 16.

Within a few short weeks, I literally fell in love with Physics, and I guess Tony sensed this too. I had already volunteered to work for the math department during my "free" period each day, but after taking my first few physics classes with Tony, decided to switch to working for the science department and help Tony prepare setting up the experiment equipment for her physics classes.

The chemistry and physics classes actually consisted of three rooms. The first was the lecture room with rows of seats that sloped upward from the front of the class to the rear. In the front of the class there was of course a blackboard and in front of it, between first row of seats and the blackboard was a granite topped table with a sink. It was on this classroom table that the physics equipment for the experiment demonstrations was set up day. My "job" as a volunteer for the physics dept. was to move the equipment each day to and from a centrally located storage area that was the second room located between the physics lab and the lecture room. This equipment was set up on the table of the lecture hall and was used by Tony on a daily basis to demonstrate the physics principles that were the subject of each days lectures.

I really enjoyed this "job" since I had a chance to operate the various pieces of equipment to ensure that they would function properly when used before an actual class.y.

There were several events that stand out in my mind that occurred while I was both a student taking physics as a junior and as Tony's private helper during my junior and senior years.

On one day, while I was helping out, and Tony was teaching a class, she was using a glass beaker and some chemicals, and while emptying the beaker, she accidentally dropped it and it fell to the floor and smashed. In the front row of this class was a red haired heavyset girl with freckles who was called "Fitzy" by everyone. Further, most of us knew that she had been "around the block" so to speak more than a few times.

When the beaker hit the floor and broke, Tony let a loud "Oh shit". Fitzy, exclaimed, without any hesitation: "Oh my virgin ears!" On hearing this, Tony quickly let out: "That's about all that's virgin!". Of course the class roared and Fitzy turned even redder than she normally was.

As second incident occurred shortly after the state of New York and revised the physics curriculum and added AM and FM radio transmission to the subjects that had to be covered in physics. On learning of this new addition, Tony was in a panic because to my surprise, she knew little if anything about radio transmission. Since she knew that I had already been "messing around" with my own AM radio transmitter at home, she asked me to give her a "primer" on the subject so that she could present it to her classes. I agreed, and sat down with her in private and taught her everything that I knew on the subject. In particular, I felt it was important for her to know the differences between AM and FM radio transmission since they are significantly different, each having their advantages and disadvantages. When the time came for her to present what I had taught her to her classes she asked me to sit in on the first class to ensure that she did a good job of presenting what I had taught her.

At the start of the class she mentioned the new subject material and indicated that I, who was sitting in the back of the class, had shared with her my knowledge on the subject. She then proceeded to discuss AM and FM radio signal transmission. The lecture went like this:

"Now class, there are two different types of radio signals that are sent by the numerous radio stations that we can listen to on our home radios".

Because she was very nervous she then blurted out the following:

"These to types of radio signals are called *AF and MF.*"

The class instinctively knew this was not correct and as everyone turned around to look at me, I slowly sank to the floor and tried to hide. It was embarrassing for both of us, and I am not sure who was more ashamed of what she had said.

The last incident came when Tony was covering the topic of static electricity and was giving a demonstration of something called a "Wimshurst Machine". This piece of equipment was a rather large affair that consisted of a large glass wheel on which were conductive copper metal discs. There was a crank that caused the disk to rotate on a central spindle and as the disc rotated metal insulated brushes that would touch the metal discs as they passed by and pick up the electrostatic charge produced by the friction. The charge that was picked up was transferred by insulated wire to two Leydon Jars that stored the charge. The stored charge in the two jars could then be used to demonstrate the effects of static electricity.

On this particular day, during my senior year, Judy, who by that time was known by all to be my girlfriend, was taking physics with Tony and was seated in the front row. After charging the two Leydon Jars, Tony, who was demonstrating the insulating effects of a small stool that had rubber legs, asked Judy to come up to the front of the class toward the insulated platform. Tony had asked me to help with the demonstration by standing on the platform and holding onto one of the Leydon Jar's electrodes. As she turned the crank of the Wimshurst Machine, and the charge built up on the jars, my hair, of which I had plenty at that time, stood up.

Tony then asked Judy to give me a kiss. As she did this, a spark jumped from my lips to Judy's as the leydon jar dumped its charge. We both were startled and the class was in an uproar. Of course, I am sure no one ever forgot this lesson relating to static electricity. To this day I still wonder if Tony had planned this "experiment" with Judy and I or whether she just thought of it during the class. In either case we all learned a good lesson about static electricity.

Interestingly, many years after moving to Pennsylvania, late in my career, I worked for a company that specialized in static electricity where, over the course of several years, I designed numerous pieces of equipment to measure the properties of materials and flooring related to static electricity. I also designed several pieces of test equipment that generated static electricity as well as test equipment to control both temperature and humidity in a sealed test chamber.

My Take On "Joe Normal"

When I was a youngster and teenager, I thought about people, their personalities and interpersonal relationships, and developed a picture in my mind regarding what I thought was normal or typical of the people around me. This picture was based on my immediate world consisting of my family (aunts, uncles, parents, siblings, etc.), my friends, my schoolmates and teachers, and the impressions created by TV, Radio, the newspapers, and the movies. I believed, earlier in my life, that people got married, and stayed that way, people cared about and helped one another, although there was a war (WWII) that started just about when I was born, that most people loved one another and wanted to live in peace, and that there was mutual respect and thoughtfulness in the workplace and world in general. Since my scope was limited to those who lived in the United States, I assumed that everyone in the world thought, felt, and behaved as we here in America did. That was my picture of what I call "Joe Normal".

As I advanced to mid-life, and had worked in the "real world" for 15 years or so as a degreed professional electronics engineer, was married, and had traveled a fair amount in the USA, my picture of "Joe Normal" began to change. For some reason, early in life, I thought of people falling on a "normal" curve that looked somewhat like the following, with Joe Normal falling in the middle at about the 50% point and representing the majority of the people.

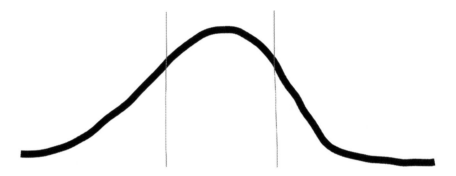

By the time I had reached about the age of 35, and I had had the opportunity to expand my horizon through the people I met and spoke to both at work and in my travels, my picture of Joe Normal had changed significantly, since I learned that my earlier beliefs were not accurate. I observed competition rather than cooperation in the workplace, hate, rather than love, and war throughout the world, rather than peace. I found that people seemed to care more about themselves rather than others, and generally did what was best for themselves with little regard for the feelings of others.

In my immediate family, my aunts, uncles and cousins who I was very close to and thought were "flawless", I learned, had many faults. I learned that my own grandmother had a sister that she had not spoken to in 25 years, and when I was about 15, one aunt and uncle divorced because my uncle was "running around" with another woman. My cousin Linda, who I was perhaps closest to among my many cousins, turned out to be a very jealous and self centered person. I discovered this when I met my first serious girl friend (who later became my wife) in high school and started going "steady". My cousin Linda, who I thought loved and cared about me, turned on me with hate because of my new found "love". She never accepted my new girl friend, and within a few months, we drifted apart, never again to become close.

In the work place, I found that there was a silent war going on in virtually every company I worked for. Instead of caring and cooperation, I found that it was management versus the worker. Even among my fellow coworkers, instead of cooperation and sharing, there was jealousy and an attitude of self protection. There was competition to get the best assignments, the best promotions, and the best raises. Tactics were often used (hard to detect or prove) by both management and my coworkers that were dishonest and self defeating in that, in the long run, I felt they cost the company real dollars because of the inefficiency that was created and time wasted.

I also began to notice that even at the national government level, there seemed to be a sense of self-serving, self-interest, that was not related to serving the public, and that was prevalent and seemed to be growing. Unfortunately, this trend seems to have continued until today.

At the present time, I am well past my prime and in the autumn of my life, and the picture of "Joe Normal" has continued to deviate from my perception as a youngster.

The statistics for marriage, as an example, are continuing to shift toward marriage becoming extinct. At the present time, depending on who you turn to for numbers on the subject, there is about a 50% likelihood that a couple marrying today, will not be together in only 10 years. We seem to be living in a throw-away society where people seem to give up on their marriages at the slightest whim. Instead of talking to one another and seeking a solution to their problems, married couples today seem to just head for the divorce courts and end it.

People today seem more concerned about themselves than those around them than they ever did in past times. This is evident on our highways, where road-rage has become the norm. Discourteous driving is also increasing where people seem to drive like there is no one else on the road but themselves. Tailgating, speeding, passing on the right, and failing to use the directional signals have become the norm rather than the exception. It can also be easily detected in our malls and supermarkets where people are less courteous about those around them then in the past.

In short, the "Joe Normal" of today is not the one I envisioned in my earlier years. Is it that I have changed and my perception is skewed, or have things actually gotten worse over the years. It is my sincere belief that I am still very objective and that things have for the most part changed for the worse.

Who is this "Joe Normal" of today?

He is one who thinks he is the only one on our planet. His world revolves about getting "stuff" and adding to it as quickly as possible. The word philosophy is not in his vocabulary. He wants a big expensive house to live in, a fancy car to drive, and wants to wear expensive "name brand" clothes, and take expensive vacations. He does not know the name of his next-door neighbor, and could care less! He does not read much, but spends 5 to 6 hours a day watching the "junk" on TV or on the internet, playing games, or keeping in touch with others via very impersonal e-mail messages that he can also "bang out" on his hand held communication devices. He is married to his cell phone and would be lost without it. He listens to radio and/or TV talk shows to "buy into" what is said and rarely does any research on his own to check out reality.

On the government level, our country is in deep trouble! The politicians of today seem to be more concerned about getting re-elected and the security and perks that come with the job, rather than doing what those who elected them want and need. They do not listen, or just go through the motions of listening, but do not act to benefit their constituents. The government keeps getting bigger, and our taxes keep increasing to support the growing numbers. The special interest groups that help them get elected are the ones that get their attention and not the people at large. This is not a pretty picture, and it is not about to get better any time soon.

So who is "Joe Normal"? Forget the normal curve. I have decided that it is a flat line, with no peak in the middle. In short, it's all out there, so just pick what you want.

What's Your Favorite Movie?

While I was still working at the Woods School in Langhorne, PA, I frequently had lunch at the on campus cafeteria with a psychologist whose name was Bob. At lunch, we discussed many things and had numerous very deep and interesting discussions. At lunch one day, he asked me a question that really stumped me. Knowing that my wife and I enjoyed watching movies, he asked me what I considered to be my favorite movie.

I am not often at a loss for words, but this one was a first, and I was not sure how to answer his question. I began to recall some of the movies I had watched over the years and began reciting those that immediately came to mind. These initial recollections included titles like:

> "Twelve Angry Men",
> "The Magnificent Seven",
> "To Kill A Mocking Bird",

"Alcatraz", and,

"Gone With The Wind".

As I rambled on, it came to me that the list goes on and on since Hollywood has turned out some great stuff since movies began over 100 years ago. Interestingly, along with the great movies, there was a lot of grade D junk that was also produced. We frequently go to our local library in Richboro, PA, and borrow DVDs to watch in the evening and too often, after starting one title or another, simply take it off because it is, in our opinion, pretty awful. We often wonder why Hollywood even produces this junk that is not worth the stuff it is recorded on.

In either case, I said to Bob that I would try to generate a list of movies that I considered great and over the next few weeks jot them down for him. I put a piece of paper in my pocket and whenever I thought of a great movie, I would jot down its title. Over the following two weeks or so, I filled up three sheets, 8 1/2 by 11 inches, both sides with those movies that I think were great. Then I stopped writing. It was not that I ran out of great movies to include, but I realized for the first time that the list is almost endless. Interestingly, my list did not include the weekly serials that I recall seeing in our local movie houses in the Bronx in the late 40's and early 50's. These would include the "Our Gang" movies, and the early "Flash Gorden" movies that were very popular back then.

I met with Bob again for lunch after starting on my best movie list, and handed him the three sheets and simply said: "Hey Bob, you really got me thinking about this stuff for the first time and I came to the conclusion that Hollywood really turned out some great movies over the years. Here is a partial list of the good stuff. Pick what you want, and enjoy. It's all very good."

The bottom line is that there are lots of great movies out there and the choices are almost endless. One should decide first on what they enjoy and whether they want to be entertained or educated since there are many documentaries out there on numerous subjects. Many documentaries are only one hour long but some run two hours or more. Some, such as those on history, have more than one episode. Some may take several nights to watch. There are also both true and fictional mysteries that are very engaging. There is also the genre of what is known as Science Fiction or "Sci-Fi".

Today, we also have choices on TV on such channels as Netflix, Hulu, and Amazon. On channels such as these, one can go back and watch movies from the silent era (before 1928), movies from the 30's, 40's and 50's and even watch weekly programs like "I Love Lucy" and "Happy Days". It's all out there. Just find what you want, sit back, relax, and enjoy.

Interestingly, my favorite movie is "The Wizard Of Oz" starring Judy Garland. My second favorite movie is one that Robin Williams did in 1999. It is the only science fiction movie he did and it is called "The Bi-Centennial Man". Even if you are not a great fan of Sci-Fi, I highly recommend you consider watching this movie. It is a very unusual movie in which Robin plays a robot that, due to a programming error is given human emotions. The plot follows him over two hundred years of his existence, from being a walking computer to being a human. If you do watch it, I would appreciate your giving me your opinion on the movie. It is so well done, that even the introduction is great.

In summary, there are almost limitless movies out there and many can be borrowed from your local library in the DVD format, and there may be no cost.

What is *your* favorite movie?

My Last Colonoscopy - An Enjoyable Experiance?

There are many things in life that are enjoyable and memorable like seeing a great movie, listening to a favorite tune, taking a great vacation, or getting together with friends and enjoying their company. Unfortunately, there are some things that we don't look forward to like having to go through the ordeal of having a stranger stick a camera up where the sun doesn't shine. This procedure is known as a Colonoscopy, and although you are "put under" (anesthetized) for it, because of the preparation and the procedure itself, one does not generally look forward to having it done.

A few years ago, I received a notice from my doctor that I was due for having a colonoscopy to ensure that everything "down there" was OK. I scheduled an appointment to have the procedure done, and got the necessary "prep" kit, that is used the day before the procedure. Most people feel that the preparation is actually worse than the procedure itself since you spend a great deal of time on the toiled after the liquid is swallowed, and it can be very messy if you don't make it to the bathroom in time.

The procedure itself only takes about 15 minutes, and is done in an outpatient department of a hospital but because of being "put under", you have to have someone with you to drive you home. Since my wife cannot drive, my daughter Cheri, accompanied me and my wife to the hospital on the morning of the procedure.

When my name was called, I went into the dressing room, got undressed and put on the surgery gown. I got onto a table and was wheeled into the procedure room. Waiting for me was the team that would assist with the procedure.

A few minutes later, a pleasant middle aged woman came in and introduced herself as the doctor who would perform the procedure. She mentioned that she was from New York City and received her medical training there as well as at Jefferson Hospital in Philadelphia. Since I was born and raised in the Bronx, we immediately "connected" and got into a lively discussion about my history in NY as well as hers. This went on for almost ten minutes and I really enjoyed talking to her. She then paused and said: "What are you here for?" I said: "A colonoscopy". She said: "Well, I am really enjoying talking to you, but we better get something done." I was then given an injection, and within a few minutes was in "la la land".

After waking up I was told to get dressed, which I did. After a short wait, the doctor came in and told me that aside from removing two small polyps that did not look suspicious, everything looked OK. She said that the polyps would be checked but that she did not expect anything to turn up. She then shook my hand and said she really enjoyed meeting and talking to me and was happy that nothing of concern was found during the procedure.

As we walked out to the parking lot to return home, I smiled, and said to my wife and daughter: "That was so much fun, I think I will come back next week and have another one done."

My Career and It's Impact on The World

When I graduated CCNY in January of 1963 and started my 43 year career as a professional electronics circuit and systems engineer, I had no way of knowing that I was embarking on a journey that would enable me to enrich the lives of many tens of thousands of people throughout the globe.

My first project as a junior engineer working for a small company in Westbury, Long Island, NY, called Digital Electronics, was to work on a new satellite launching program called the Orbiting Astronomical Observatory, or OAO for short. The concept was to launch an earth satellite and place it outside of the earths atmosphere so that clear pictures of "what is out there" (in space) could be photographed. You have probably never heard of the OAO, but a few years after the launch of three OAO satellites, another satellite, launched in 1990 was known throughout the world. This well known satellite was known as the Hubble Telescope. The OAO was its predecessor.

While at Digital, I also worked on one of the very early computer systems that we were developing for the community colleges in NY. It had no display as we know it today, but used an IBM Selectric typewriter as the input/output device (keyboard and display). It used a rotating magnetic drum as the memory device since the integrated circuit memories that are commonly used today, had not yet come along. The system was very slow, did use solid state technology, but was very slow and limited by today's standards.

I left Digital Electronics two years later and joined the Sperry Gyroscope Company in Great Neck, Long Island. Although there for only three months, I worked on a state of the art system for the City of New York known as TRACKS. It was a computer based system that was tied into the traffic light system in the five boroughs. The idea was to monitor the traffic moving through the city using cameras located on strategic street corners, feed this information into a central computer, and control the traffic light patterns to optimize the traffic flow. My contribution was to design a standby timer system to take over in the event of a power failure so that traffic would not come to a standstill during the power outage.

I left Sperry and then joined a company called EDO, in College Point NY, next to the Whitestone Bridge. While there, I worked on DC to DC conversion circuits and systems and developed quite a bit of unique knowledge regarding converting voltages from one level to another and from DC to AC at efficiencies that were unheard of at the time. While at EDO, I was assigned to a project to help solve a problem on a state of the art sonar system known as the AN/SQS 26BX Sonar. It was being developed for the US Navy Department and had hit a snag that brought production literally to a halt because a tiny relay about one inch high was failing at random and no one knew why. My supervisor, assigned me to this problem, and although

I hadn't a clue regarding what was causing this tiny relay to fail, or how to repair it, I managed to design a unique new system that would test this failing component and enable the potentially bad ones to be weeded out before they caused a catastrophic failure resulting in hundreds of thousands of wasted dollars and wasted man hours. Within six months of being assigned to this problem, I managed to come up with a solution and literally "saved the day". Needless to say, I became an instant hero, got a raise and promotion, but then left the company because of a desire to leave New York, and work in a totally unrelated (non military) field know as *Biomedical Engineering*. Everyone at EDO was shocked when I tendered by resignation, but there was nothing they could offer me since they worked strictly on Sonar Systems for the Navy. So we packed up with our to year old daughter Joy, and left New York for Trevose, Pennsylvania.

After moving to eastern Pennsylvania, I worked for eight more companies over the nest forty years and did some of the best work of my career.

I helped develop a wireless EKG monitoring system during my first year in the Biomedical Engineering field. In the mid-seventies, I managed the team that developed advanced encryption software that was applied to the voice communication system for the NASA Space Shuttle. I also managed the team that advanced the software and hardware that made virtually everything that uses advanced microcircuits including cell phones and anything that uses complicated integrated circuits, possible.

I also designed some unique circuits that were used by the Boeing company in the development of the 757 and 767 aircraft.

I worked in the electrostatics field and designed over 20 unique products that put numbers on various materials related to how they act when they become electrostatically charged.

My last job was in the special needs field when I started and managed the Assistive Technology Department for a large not-for-profit company in Lower Bucks County. I retired from this, my last full time job, but still provided technical services for private clients with special needs. I still work with one client that I have been working with for over 25 years.

Virtually everything I worked on during my long career, helped make the world better and helped tens of thousands, if not millions of people live better lives. The space shuttle in particular, because of the thousands of products that were developed as a result of this program, helped enrich the lives of people world wide. I call this "fall out" but it actually represents things developed as byproducts of the actual program and its flights.

My most directly fulfilling job however was when I worked in the special needs field since I was working with both the clients and staff to enrich the lives of those I worked with by applying my skills and technology that was available.

Interestingly, my four and a half years studying electrical engineering at CCNY was free. My only cost was to purchase my books and a lab coat. The total cost was about six hundred dollars.

Necessity Is The Mother Of Invention: The Stuff I Invented

I never planned on inventing anything, but as you go through life, things happen, in many cases not planned, and ones mind begins to churn out ideas. In most cases, in my opinion anyway, inventions are born because of some problem that pops up that is looking for a solution.

With me, it all started in December of 1964 while my wife and 9 month old daughter Joy were living on Hull Avenue in the Bronx, about 3 months after I had purchased our first new car. It was a Chevy Bel Air station wagon, a bottom of the line model. I even ordered it without a radio, since we literally had no money to spare. I recall purchasing a radio through the mail and building a case for it so that I could install it under the dash board. I still have the radio in its original case.

It was Xmas day, and I had parked our new Chevy right in front of our third floor apartment overnight. I went down in the morning to buy some rolls at Butterflake Bakery on Gun Hill Road and pick up the Sunday paper. As I walked past our car, I noticed that the wing window on the driver side of the front seat was open. This was odd, since I never left the car unattended with the window open. I unlocked the car and slid into the drivers seat to close the window when I noticed that it had been pried open and was no longer connected to the crank handle that was used to open and close the manual window. I also noticed that there were foot prints on the front seat and that the cover to the spare tire was partially open. Clearly, someone had tried to break into my car and steal the spare tire. Luckily, the spare tire was still there, but a pair of winter gloves that I had left on the front seat, were gone.

Needless to say, I had this feeing for the first time in my life, that my rights as an individual had been violated. I had never experienced anything like this before, and was angry that someone would do such a thing. After breakfast I drove the car to my parents home about three miles away, and installed a locking bracket on the spare tire cover and locked the cover in place with a small key access lock. I also taped the broken window shut with some tape so that it would not get wet in the car if it rained.

Exactly one week later, on New Years morning, what happened on Xmas day was repeated, however, instead of getting in through the taped (broken) window, the thieves pried the wing window on the passenger side of the front seat open to get in. I suspect it was the same people who broke into the car on Xmas eve. They must have been shocked to find the spare tire cover with a lock. This time they did not get anything since there was nothing of value to easily take. This second incident, just a short week after the first, was what really got my dander up.

This event, the breaking in to my car, two times in just one week, resulted in my giving the problem some serious thought. Within a few days, I conceived the idea of designing a low cost theft prevention system that could be easily installed on any car that would provide an audible and visual warning if an unauthorized person entered a car on which the system was installed and activated. Within a few short days, I had designed a very tiny electronic module that I later named "Car Guard", that could be purchased for less than twenty dollars, and installed on any car or truck in just an hour using a few simple tools.

This unit could be installed with a fender mounted arming lock switch that would arm or disarm the system with a turn of a simple key. I designed the system so that simple mercury tilt switches could be added to the system to protect the engine compartment and trunk as well as the interior of the car or truck.

I took my efforts a step further, and after some research, decided to apply for a patent on my new system. In about a year, a patent was granted to cover my Car Guard system. Unfortunately, I never made any money on my idea because I knew virtually nothing about marketing and even if I did, I had no money to pay for someone to market the system for me. I did sell a few units to an owner of a fleet of trucks, but never made enough in sales to cover the cost of the patent.

Although I am proud of my invention and the patent, unfortunately, it never amounted to much in the way of profits. Today, whenever someone approaches me with a new idea and wants to go further, I always ask: "What is your marketing plan". What I learned from Car Guard was the simple truth that having an idea in America and making a few dollars on it are two entirely different things. Also, the success or failure of a good idea depends not so much on the idea, but how it is marketed. About twenty years later, I had another great idea and invented a unique garden tool that I named *Wonder Weeder*.

Wonder Weeder was invented because, as an avid gardener, I was tired of having to carry several garden tools with me each time I went out to plant, cultivate, and weed. Further, because of the many flower beds I had including a rock garden, where the lawn met a flower bed, none of the tools I had could be used to maintain an edge. Wonder Weeder can do seven different things including restoring an edge to be a sharp as the edge of a table.

History will prove that my experiences are not unique regarding inventing new things. Problems need solutions, and inventions most often result because of a problem that needs a solution.

Our Cabin In The Woods

In the summer of 1989 we made a decision that changed our lives.

For about four years, since about 1985, we had been spending our Memorial Day weekends visiting with some friends who had a small cabin in the Pocono Mountains of Pennsylvania. Each May, we would gather at their home in Pocono Pines with several of our other mutual friends, and spend the weekend socializing at their cabin in a community known as *Lake Naomi*. If the weather permitted, we would cook outdoors on a BBQ pit, eat hamburgers, chicken and hot dogs, and sit around just talking and having a great time. Of course, we took little nips of wine or stronger stuff just to round off the edges so to speak.

By 1989, we had enjoyed our get-togethers so much that we had literally fallen in love with *Lake Naomi* and the quieter life that it provided. We started looking for a suitable place to buy earlier that year, but nothing exciting that fit our needs and wants came up. In August of 89', the real estate broker we had been working with found a small cabin that they felt we might like. We made an appointment to see it and although very small, we felt that it might fit the bill. Unfortunately, major reconstruction of the support beams in the crawl space was underway when we arrived, so we toured the cabin then, since we were on our way to Canada for our summer vacation, we told the realtors that we would think about the place and make a decision while we were away.

When we returned in two weeks, we met again with the realtors but were told that another family had seen the place and had put down a deposit. We left somewhat disappointed, but decided to keep looking.

About a month later, we had all but forgotten about our little cabin in *Lake Naomi* when the phone rang. It was the realtor, calling to inform us that the couple that had placed the deposit on the cabin couldn't get a mortgage. We said that we were still interested and would look at it again and make a decision on the spot. The repair work had been completed and we checked both the crawl space and the interior and decided that we would take it.

Coincidentally, we had also looked at a lot near Camelback Mountain and had decided to purchase it as an investment. This decision, it turned out, was a bad call. At the time of this writing, almost 28 years later, we still own the lot, and would be lucky to get half of what we paid for it. But that is another story.

We closed on the cabin and the lot in December of 1989 and after closing, stayed at the cabin that night. Our daughter Sandi, was with us and we all enjoyed our new "get away" place. Since it was sold completely furnished, all we needed for our nights stay was some fresh clothes for the next day, linens for the beds and a few towels. It was a nice start to what turned out to be one of the best decisions we had ever made.

We have been using our cabin now for about 28 years, and since it is electrically heated, it is a cinch to open and close each time we use it. We don't have to worry about oil or gas deliveries, and in the winter, we keep the thermostats in the living room and bathroom at about 45 degrees to keep the pipes from freezing. Our two largest costs are the taxes and electric bill. We use the cabin about every other week most of the time but in the summer we use it almost every weekend. When I retired in 2006, our stays extended from two days, usually over the weekends, to whenever we want to get away and for however long we want to stay.

Some fringe benefits to our get away place included the Blakeslee Diner in Blakeslee, where we had breakfast almost every Saturday when we visit our little get away place. Another great diversion is the flea market right next to the Blakeslee Diner where we always stop after breakfast and usually find some goody or two to add to our collection of "stuff". I have purchased many LP records there that have added to our enjoyment of the world's great music. If the timing is right, we also stop at much larger flea market in Saylorsburg where we also usually find a thing or two to add to our "stuff".

Another fringe benefit to our cabin in the casino at the old Mount Airy Lodge, that was completely rebuilt. We go there a few times a year to have a few hours of fun at the slots and make our donation to the state part of which goes to help needy seniors.

We often cook out on a makeshift stone fire place I assembled many years ago out of stone that is abundant on our ½ acre property. I love cooking out on this grille since I feel like a cowboy being in the woods and very close to nature.

I have put together a nice audio system so that we can enjoy listening to records, CD's, and cassette tapes. Although we don't have cable TV, I rigged up an outside antenna that a friend gave us, so that we can catch the news and weather via an off the air tuner. We have a decent TV set so that we can watch DVD's that we borrow from the local library or the one at home or watch stuff that I pick up at the flea markets.

I also rigged up a small PC in one corner so that I can type away, like I am now doing. I have written about 100 or so memoirs here on this computer, and am having a ball. I also work on my Power Point presentations here most of the time since I have the Office suite installed with Word and Power Point. I also do my landscape paintings here on a small table on our open deck when the weather is warm or inside on our kitchen table.

We also play scrabble and a card game called "Five Crowns" or just sit around and read or do Suduco puzzles.

The bottom line is that our little "cabin in the woods" has not only been a life changer and a life saver, but has expanded our horizons regarding the activities that we engage in. Oh yes, before I forget, my wife Judy wrote a unique cookbook here that is a collection of 547 of the best recipes covering 30 nationalities of food. It was published by Morris Cookbooks.

I have come to the realization that our little get away place has given us literally two lives: one at our primary residence in Newtown, and one here in the woods at our little cabin. It has been a life saver.

"Out Of The Mouths Of Babes"

A true, very funny, short story

When my granddaughter Morgan was only about 4 years old, she was accompanying my daughter Cheri as they did their weekly shopping at a local supermarket in Richboro, Pa, near where they lived.

My daughter Cheri was walking up and down the isles pushing a shopping cart, and Morgan, who was only about 2 ½ feet tall at the time, was walking along side her as they did their shopping.

As they finished the isle they had been shopping in and turned the corner to enter the next isle, Morgan looked up and notice a "rather large" woman with a shopping cart, also making her way up and down the food isles filling her cart with items that she needed.

Upon seeing this "rather large" woman, Morgan, who was outspoken and very uninhibited, quietly and without Cheri noticing, left her side, and walked up to this strange woman, looked her straight in the eye and politely said: "Boy lady, you are fat."

Morgan, being very young and not realizing that she had just released a virtual hand grenade, nonchalantly turned and quietly walked back to where her mother Cheri, was shopping. Cheri who could not help but watch and hear what had just happened, was beyond embarrassed and was probably in somewhat of a state of shock, to put it very mildly.

Cheri quickly took Morgan by the hand and walked some distance from where the "rather large" woman was shopping, and when they were out of hearing range of the other woman, said to Morgan: "Why did you say that to that strange woman?" Morgan, who could not figure out what was happening, wide eyed and innocently looking, turned to Cheri and replied; "Mommy, she is very fat." Cheri then proceeded to explain to Morgan that there are some things that even if they are true, should not be said, particularly to a total stranger

They continued wandering up and down the isles of the supermarket to finish their shopping, and finally ended up at the checkout counter. Cheri pushed her cart with Morgan close by into the next available checkout lane and proceeded to start placing her purchases on the conveyer belt to be scanned by the checkout clerk. Just as she started to place the first few items on the checkout belt, the "rather large" woman, who Morgan had spoken so rudely to, got onto the same checkout lane right behind them.

Cheri, hoping to repair some of the damage, and wanting to further teach Morgan proper behavior, leaned down to Morgan and said very quietly; "Morgan, I think it would be nice for you to go over to that nice woman and apologize for what you said to her back there a few minutes ago." Little, innocent looking Morgan, without hesitating, simply took a few short steps toward the woman behind them in the checkout isle, looked her quietly in the eye and said; "Lady, I am very sorry for what I said to you back there in the store while we were shopping." She paused for a few seconds......................then added: "But you really are fat!"

Our Little Dog Winky

081219

Things in life often happen in strange ways. How we got our little puppy Winky is one of those strange and interesting stories. He arrived suddenly and the one who gave him to me ran off before I could say anything. We all fell in love with him and he became a family member for the next 16 years. Here is Winky's story.

After moving from the Bronx in the late summer of 1966, we lived in a garden apartment in Trevose Pennsylvania, just north of Philadelphia. After settling in we quickly made friends with virtually all of the folks who lived in our apartment complex. Living in the apartment just next to us was a couple about our age who we had become very friendly with.

In the fall of 1967, our new custom built home in Churchville, about 10 minutes from where our garden apartment was, was finished, and we moved in. During that year, we made many trips back to our old garden apartment to visit with our friends there. That fall, our friends from next door in the garden apartment had just gotten a little puppy and we played with him while we were visiting there. Our daughter Joy, who was about 3 ½ years old, immediately fell in love with this cute little black mixed breed puppy that was all black except for a little bit of white hair under his little chin. This puppy was only about two weeks old and clearly was not house broken yet.

After visiting for a few hours, we said goodbye, got into our 1964 Chevy station wagon, and left for our new home in Churchville. Our daughter Joy seemed extremely quiet during our short trip home. We suspected that she had become attached to the cute little puppy our friends had just gotten.

We were home only a few minutes when the doorbell rang. When I opened it there was Barbara, our friend, standing with tears in her eyes, holding her cute little puppy. Before I could say anything, she abruptly said: "Here, he's yours", and literally shoved the little guy into my hands. She abruptly turned, got into her car, and drove off. I was left speechless, standing at my front door, with this tiny little thing just staring lovingly up at me.

I closed the door and behind me was my wife Judy, quietly staring at me and what I was holding. She said: "Who was that?". I replied: "It was Barbara, and it looks like we have a new member of our family." A few seconds later, Joy came running over and saw the little cute puppy in my arms. She reached out and took it with love in her eyes. They immediately "connected". In fact, we all fell in love with our new dog. It did not take long for Joy to pick a nice name for our new pet. She named him Winky.

Winky turned out to be a great pet who learned things very quickly, was obedient, and a great traveler. We took him virtually everywhere we went. When traveling by car and staying at one or more motels, as soon as we entered our room for the night, he ran in, found a nice quiet corner, and just made himself at home. In the car, he would crawl up at Judy's feet and was very quiet. Of course, we had to make stops while on the road to let Winky "do his thing" but this was no problem. He came with us on every vacation we took to Rangely Maine and stayed with us in our housekeeping cottage. He even went with us in Rangeley to pick blueberries. He would run ahead of us seek out a nice low bush blueberry plant, and nibble away at the fresh blueberries.

As time went by, we all got older and one day we had to make a very difficult decision to have Winky put to sleep. He had reached the ripe old age of about 16 but had lost most of his hearing, had developed cancer and was having trouble walking. Toward the end, he could not go into the backyard of our home in Churchville to "do his thing", so in the mornings, we usually found a nice "present", that Winky invariable left, always on a small rug in our family room where he slept.

We could see that he was in pain, even though he did not "complain", and it became clear to all of us (we were now a family of five), that Winky was no longer enjoying life. As a result, Judy and I decided that his time had come, so we found a pet clinic in Bucks County that would administer a shot and put Winky out of his misery. Our three children were not with us because we didn't want them to experience the pain of what we had to do. I could not bear to bring him into the vet, so Judy agreed to do it. We did ask if they could find a home for him, but they clearly indicated that because of his age and condition, it was unlikely that they could find someone that would take him. We drove sadly away, knowing that Winky would no longer be on this planet by the end of the day.

In retrospect, it was a happy ending since we "adopted" a cut little puppy who spent the next 16 years as part of our family. He was a wonderful dog who gave us a great deal of joy. I suspect, that if he could speak, he would say that we were also the ideal family for him.

My Girlfriend Renay & How
I Learned To Dance

11/6/2015

It was September of 1952, and I had just finished grade school at P.S 87 in the northeast Bronx, New York. The city of New York had recently introduced a new concept in education, the Junior High School. Up until the 1950's there were basically just grade schools, where a student started in Kindergarten, and progressed from there through grades 1 to 8, spending a total of 9 years at the same "grade school". When the junior high school was introduced, it was intended to be an intermediate step from grade school to high school. It was a very good idea since students were able to take classes that were not offered in grade school such as woodworking, sheet metal working, sewing, homemaking (cooking things and preparing food), and something called social dancing. It was this last class that I took in the 9th grade, my final year in Junior High School, that is the topic of this article.

In the 9th grade, I had science, english, math, history, foreign language (Spanish), and social dancing. This last class was held in the school's auditorium where we all gathered on the stage while music was played from records and the sound was heard over a loudspeaker system in the auditorium. It was in the 8th grade at Olinville Junior High School, also known as PS 113, on Olinville Avenue, that I developed a "crush" on a girl whose name was Renay

Renay was a classmate of mine in class 8-2. She lived about ½ mile from where I lived on Murdock Avenue with my parents and a brother and sister who were 5 and 11 years younger than I was. Renay, if I recall was an only child who was also learning to play the piano when I met her when I had just turned 12 in August of that summer. She was about my height, perhaps an inch or so smaller, and was fairly pretty. I took a liking to her some time in the 8th grade, but nothing much came of it until we progressed to the ninth grade and both entered class 9-2. Our homeroom teacher was a Mrs. Rand who also taught science.

About 3 times a week, usually toward the end of the school day, we would gather in the auditorium and a teacher would help us learn the basic steps of the popular dances of the day. In those days the so called dancing that people do today were unknown. Today, people get up and "jump around" on the dance floor waving their hands and shaking their bodies and seldom, if ever, hold their dancing partners. The dances that people did in the 1950's were the Fox Trot, Lindy, Rumba, Tango, Waltz, and the Cha-Cha. This last dance, the Cha-Cha, became my favorite that I still love to dance to even today. I also enjoy doing the Lindy (also known as the Lindy Hop), but because it is very strenuous, it is getting more and more difficult for me to dance from start to finish of a given dance number. One of my favorite Lindys was Bill Haley's "Rock-Around-The-Clock". Bill

Haley, and his group were known as "The Comets", and they were one of the most popular small dance bands of the 1950's.

We recently went on a day trip sponsored by our local senior center to Doolan's a popular catering place at the Jersey Shore. The trip to Doolan's featured a full sit-down lunch, a comedian who had us in stitches, and an orchestra that played dance music from the 50's and 60's. One of the bands performers was a man whose last name was Turner, who played the electric guitar, said he actually played with Bill Haley's Comets in the 50's and 60's. It was a real treat for us when the band played Rock-Around-The-Clock and we had a chance to do the Lindy with Turner playing this classic Rock and Roll song from so long ago.

When I took social dancing at Olinville, Renay and I always chose to be dance partners. We learned to do all of the above noted dances together, and over the course of a year while we were in the 9th grade, we became quite good at it. Unfortunately, when we went on to Evander Childs High School, the following year, there was no social dancing class. That is the bad news. The good news however, was that in the fall of 1955, when I had just turned 15, I met another girl who I later fell in love with and ultimately married. Fortunately, she too had learned how to dance before me met and we went on through our lives to dance the social or ball room style dances we had both learned in our early teen years, she in grade school and me at JHS 113. Clearly, when I met Judy at Evander, my relationship with Renay passed into the background and my early crush on her disappeared. Later in life, Renay and I rekindled our friendship, but only at a distance since she had moved to south Florida, and I was living with Judy and my family in Churchville Pennsylvania.

I am very happy that I learned social (ballroom) dancing early in my life since it has given Judy and I a great deal of pleasure to be able to get up on a dance floor, and "do our thing" provided the band was playing something we could recognize and dance to. During our recent trip to Doolans we often got compliments from other seniors who admired our ability to dance, particularly the Cha-Cha and Lindy. A fringe benefit of being able do these dances, is that they are both good cardio-vascular exercises, so in addition to having fun, we are also contributing to keeping our bodies agile and in shape.

So folks, don't just sit there and read my book. Get off your duff and dance!

The Best Years of My Professional Career as an Electronics Engineer

In looking over my long career as an electronics circuit and systems designer, it is hard for me to single out the best years of my career since from my leaving CCNY in January of 1963 with my bachelors degree in EE and starting work in industry to my retirement 43 years later, I can't honestly find a time that I was not doing challenging and creative work. There were however, a few projects that stand out as exceptional.

In the mid 1970's, while working for General Atronics, Inc., a Subsidiary of the Magnavox Corp., then part of NV Philips of the Netherlands, I had the opportunity to head the team that designed the voice communication system for the NASA Space Shuttle. On my team were three other engineers who were exceptional individuals both because of their credentials and experience. One member of the team was a top notch digital designer, who, earlier in his career, worked at the University of Pennsylvania in Phila, and was part of the team that developed the ENIAC, the world's first digital computer. Another member of the team, who did most of the programming related to testing the completed system, was a young digital engineer named Mike. A third engineer whose specialty was also digital design was also a young designer was also named Mike. The two Mike's did not get along and I had major problems keeping them "in line". I was the team leader and analog designer of the system. Fortunately, I was able to keep the team working fairly smoothly and the job was successfully completed. When we delivered the first system of the 20 that we built and delivered to NASA, we flew to Mission Control in Houston Texas, where the acceptance testing was performed to ensure that the system performed according to the very complex and detailed NASA specifications. We completed all of the testing in about 3 hours and the system was accepted by NASA. We were told on completion, that we were the only contractor on this program that had delivered on time and they seemed to be amazed that the system passed without a flaw. After completing the acceptance test, we were given the grand tour of the Mission Control Center including the duplicate mission control center that is separated from the first one by 6 feet of reinforced concrete. The redundancy was needed because, according to NASA, if something were to happen to the control room, the Shuttle could not be brought back to land on earth.

I also worked on a program for the Navy called the LSI Codem. A major contributor to this effort had developed a complex digital data encoding algorithm that encrypted or scrambled digital data before it was transmitted to keep unwanted sources from receiving and processing the transmitted data. Codem stands for coding and demodulation. It actually had two parts, one for coding (encryption) and the second for decoding (decryption). The voice signals were first converted to digital ones and zeroes. Once digitized the voice signal was encrypted. If I recall, there was one part known as LINK 11, which was being developed for the Navy and was a fairly simple algorithm that consisted of a 4X4 data matrix that after coding resulted in a 5X5 bit matrix. The more complex part encoded a 5 X 5 bit matrix and resulted in a 36 bit encoded matrix. A major part of the program was to use a new technology called LSI for Large Scale Integration to enable the digital portions of the system to be manufactured on silicon wafers that were 2.2" in diameter. GAC was the prime contractor on this program and Hughes Aircraft, in Culver City, CA, was a subcontractor on this program. I was the manager that had to manage the whole program including the work doing done by Hughes. What I did not know at the time was that this pioneering work was to lay the foundation for integrated circuit technology that was to make things like laptops, PC's, hand held phones and notebook computers, and virtually all electronic devices made after the mid 1970's, possible.

I left GAC in the spring of 1978 to join a company in Lansdale called the American Electronics Company, or AEL for short. My plans in joining AEL related to doing state of the art development work that would make them the worlds leader in high efficiency power conversion systems. The technology that I wanted to develop would make many power converters that at the time were wasting as much as 70% of the energy they consumed to much more efficient systems that would waste as little as only 5 to 10% and convert the rest to useable energy. AEL had their own magnetics department capable of making transformers of all kinds and their own in house PC department. They also had a major sales and marketing department that would be instrumental in getting the supplies that I hoped to design to market. Unfortunately, I was seriously "sidetracked" several times during my stay at AEL and never got to work on what I joined the company for. Luckily I did land one contract that resulted in my designing some highly specialized circuits that were used for the flight test program for the Boeing 756 and 757. I ended up leaving the company under less than ideal circumstances. The good news is that as a result of my involuntarily leaving AEL, I started my own consulting company known as Noran Technical Consultants, that led to me stumbling into a completely new field known as Electrostatics. I worked in this relatively little known and relatively new field for 13 years.

I was fortunate in that I was never bored at any time during my career from 1963 until I retired in 2006, and had the opportunity to do creative work that helped make the world a better place. My last position, was perhaps the most fulfilling, was applying my talents by designing equipment to help individuals with special needs. I entered this field in 1995 and retired from it in 2006. I still provide support services for a special needs individual for whom who I have been providing services now for over 25 years.

The Elephant and the Flea

11/14/15

Many years ago, I came to the conclusion that because of the wide spread in people's personalities and the fact that there will always be a small number of people who are extreme in their beliefs and thinking, there will continue to be acts of terrorism. As a result, there will be damage to otherwise peaceful communities and the people in those communities will continue to suffer pain and death.

Yesterday, Nov 13, 2015, while I was taking a short walk, I decided to stop into a neighbors home and drop off a list of the topics that I cover in the presentations I give to various local organizations. These talks cover many topics including Space Travel and The Possibility of Extraterrestrial Life, Marilyn Monroe, and Our Energy Options, and Robin Williams. When I arrived at my neighbors home, he happened to have his TV on and while we were talking, the news of the shootings in Paris, France, broke. We sat there and watched as the newscaster revealed some of the early information regarding this horrific event.

It is now Saturday morning, November 14th, and we turned on our TV to get the latest information on this latest terrorist attic on innocent, peaceful citizens of Paris.

127 people in six different areas in Paris were killed and the number of injured is still unkown. There were at least six terrorists that either committed suicide or were killed by the French police. They were still looking for additional terrorists that may not have revealed themselves.

What disturbs me the most is that this is not the first act of terrorism and unfortunately, I believe it will not be the last.

In September of 2001, on 9/11, three planes hit the World Trade Center in New York, and within the next two hours, the damage caused by these terrorist guided planes, resulted in the total destruction of the WTC along with close to 3,000 people losing their lives. In addition there are millions of people who suffered mental damage, and a smaller number who were affected by the dust that filled the air when the towers collapsed. There was a fourth terrorist guided plane that was headed for Washington, that crashed in Western PA as a result of passengers who decided to try to stop the terrorists.

When 9/11 occurred, I knew that this was just the beginning of major terrorist activities that would cause injury, destruction and death in the future.

We, the innocent peaceful people of the world, represent the "elephant" and the terrorists represent the "flea" on the elephant. The elephant is easy to see, while the flea on the elephant is virtually invisible, and impossible to find. The terrorists know that they can easily hide until they are ready to do their evil deeds. All they have to do is wait and plan while the elephant goes about peacefully and unsuspectingly. I was certain that it was just a matter of time before the flea would strike again. The event in Paris last night was that event, and unfortunately, the fleas are still there. They will lie dormant until the elephant again becomes complacent. At the right time and place for them, they will strike again. Will it be in some foreign country or will it be right here in the United States? We can just wait and see, however, there is an option.

I am very sorry that the U.S. and the peaceful nations of the world have not taken greater steps to seek out and try to eradicate these terrorist "fleas" that will do their evil work as we go forward. I know it is hard to find the flea on the elephant, but I also believe that we, the peaceful nations of the world, have the resources to seek out and destroy these evil fleas. What are we waiting for? We have the weapons and the agencies like the CIA, that can find where these terrorists are hiding, and eliminate them from society before they strike again. Why do we rise up just after such events, and then in a relatively short time, so it seems, become lulled into complacency. This is what the terrorists want and know will happen. We have to keep our guard up, and stay on their trails until we find them and place them in jails or eliminate them before they eliminate us.

The Unsung Heroes of
the Modern World

June 12, 2023

There was a time, thousands of years ago, when mankind consisted of many small tribes that were spread over the earth, and in most cases were isolated from one another. The people of that time lived in caves or small huts made of wood, straw, sand or clay. To just survive, they had to depend on one another for food, shelter, and protection from wild animals. They were the hunters and gatherers of the early age of man.

As the worlds' population grew, the structure of civilization began to change so that man had more time to think and create ways to make life easier and safer. Man came to the realization that it was more efficient for some to specialize in providing food, for others protection, and for others to build and maintain the structures that provided protection for the elements. We gradually evolved into those who grew food (farmers), those who looked for animals to kill and eat (hunters), those who provided clothing for warmth (tailors), those who designed, built and maintained the dwellings that man lived in (builders and architects), and many others who provided man with what he needed to live and survive in comfort.

To keep things running in harmony, a system of payment for goods and services gradually evolved from one based on bartering(exchanging goods and services as payment) into one which was based on payment in an agreed upon system of money whose value was determined by a complex system, that eventually became almost impossible to understand. To earn the money needed to pay for things, people did work for others and were rewarded for their efforts by payment in terms of money (wages).

As things proceeded, the world became more and more complex. In the mid-eighteenth century, something called the industrial revolution took place during which the complexity of things took a giant leap forward. Machines were created to accomplish tasks that made getting things done easier and more efficient. A system of factories evolved in which people worked with machines to make many things that previously were made by hand using tedious and time consuming methods. People were paid in money (wages) for their work in these factories.

In the twentieth century, another revolution took place known as the technological revolution. The prelude to the technological revolution occurred in the late nineteenth century when batteries were developed that could store energy and produce something called electricity. This was followed with the development of electric motors, generators, and the electric light bulb. The discovery and development of the electric light bulb in itself was a revolution since up till that time, light was produced by burning oil and candles.

A new breed of people evolved who were the ones who worked with these new technological innovations on their further improvement, application, and maintenance. They were called engineers and scientists. Although they existed in small numbers, prior to the technological revolution, by the twentieth century, they became the ones who helped mankind take a giant leap forward. Their efforts resulted in the development of the vacuum tube, radio, television, the transistor, the integrated circuit, the computer, and the internet. Their breed also was responsible for the development and mass production of the automobile, and the airplane. Schools began turning out large numbers of these intelligent beings so that they could enter the work force, and help create new and exciting "things" to further increase man's ability to live in safety and comfort and to provide a form of entertainment to occupy man's leisure time, something that he did not have much of in earlier times.

Unfortunately, this new breed of thinkers and innovators were to pay a heavy price for their efforts.

Two elements in the nature of man that can create problems for those with exceptional creative talents are the ego and jealousy. For too many individuals, the ability to appreciate what others are capable of creating that they cannot is lacking. Their egos and jealousy prevent them from doing this. The result in many cases is a lack of appreciation for what others have created or accomplished. Further, those who lack these abilities often go out of their way to try to discredit or "bring down" the creative ones. This conflict can manifest itself in many ways and circumstances. At work for example, in companies with poor management, the creative ones are not given the recognition they deserve or the salary rewards that should match their contributions. Often, the management of the company and those in sales and marketing receive the greatest rewards (highest salaries, best promotions, etc.), while those who are actually creating what the managers manage and what the sales people sell, receive significantly lesser rewards. When the "hard times" come, and sales fall off, it is often the creative ones who pay the heavy price of losing their jobs rather than those in management, marketing or sales. This unfair practice of "punishing" the creative ones continues to exist even today.

An additional price that the creative ones pay, is a lack of recognition in many cases for what they have created. In addition, when something does not work out as planned, it is often the creative ones who are blamed for the failures when often it is the managers who are responsible for creating the problem through faulty management decisions.

I have been of the opinion, that the engineers and scientists of our time are the unsung heroes, that do not receive the recognition and credit that they deserve. We have a secretaries day, mothers day, fathers day, labor day, memorial day, veterans day, and even a day to recognize a rodent called groundhogs day, but we do not have a single day or minute to recognize those who create things and make a better world for us all. We need a day or week to recognize the creative ones who make so much possible for the rest of us. Let's think about another day to be added to those that already exist. Let's call it technology day or week to recognize and give thanks to those who have made our lives better through their efforts.

Printed in the United States
by Baker & Taylor Publisher Services